GLOBAL POSITIONING For FINANCIAL SERVICES

GLOBAL POSITIONING For FINANCIAL SERVICES

Hazel J. Johnson

Distinguished University Scholar
University of Louisville
Louisville, Kentucky, USA

World Scientific
Singapore • New Jersey • London • Hong Kong

Published by

World Scientific Publishing Co. Pte. Ltd.

P O Box 128, Farrer Road, Singapore 912805

USA office: Suite 1B, 1060 Main Street, River Edge, NJ 07661

UK office: 57 Shelton Street, Covent Garden, London WC2H 9HE

British Library Cataloguing-in-Publication Data
A catalogue record for this book is available from the British Library.

GLOBAL POSITIONING FOR FINANCIAL SERVICES

ISBN 981-02-4246-8

This book is printed on acid-free paper.

Printed in Singapore by Uto-Print

In loving memory of

Lucille V. Johnson

whose life of dignity and grace is a perpetual inspiration

Preface

The commercial banking industry is currently undergoing important structural and competitive changes. In the United States, pressure is being felt from nonbank financial sectors and from foreign banks operating within the United States. Because of bank failures and mergers, the banking industry has consolidated from 15,000 U.S. institutions to less than 9,000 in a matter of a few years. The traditional deposit-taking and lending activities are being deemphasized, as bankers search for fee-generating market niches that will supply as much as one half of their operating income. However, past regulatory constraints limited bank access to many potentially profitable lines of business such as securities and insurance.

Global Positioning in Financial Services sorts out the dynamics of the banking industry in the United States, Canada, the United Kingdom, Germany, France, Switzerland, Japan, and China, while describing current banking practices and future market trends. Compelling regulatory issues are contrasted in the United States and abroad. In this context, possible market niches and synergies for commercial banks are identified and explored.

These and other opportunities may be exploited not only by the large, multinational banks, but also by ambitious regional banks. Even in the context of constraining regulations, U.S. institutions can capitalize on their comparative strengths. Through strategic alliances, commercial banks are being transformed into internationally competitive providers of a wide range of financial services.

Contents

1. Transformation in Financial Services

Introduction

Financial services firms facilitate economic growth in modern society by performing essential functions. In the past, each firm had a narrow band of services that it offered to its consumer and business clients. The payments system was controlled by commercial banks that cleared checks and drafts. Today money is transferred electronically among any number of financial firms in volumes that could never be efficiently handled in the physical form. Residential mortgage finance was available primarily from savings and loan associations that held the loans to maturity. This mortgage finance is now available from a wide array of sources and the mortgage loans themselves are traded as securities. Securities firms offered corporate and government securities as investment vehicles. Now these firms offer close substitutes for bank deposits and help industrial firms bypass the commercial banking system in their pursuit of short-term financing. The mainstay for insurance companies was the traditional whole life insurance policy. Today insurance companies provide offer products that compete with investments obtainable through securities firms. Mutual funds have emerged to permanently change the dynamics of the banking industry.

Over time, traditional roles have been blurred and it is not always easy to distinguish the product of a commercial bank from that of another financial institution. The competitive forces in the banking industry are not limited to domestic firms. There is increased pressure from foreign institutions. The financial services industry is in the process of significant change in a time of new alignments in domestic markets and increased international competition.

The Traditional Roles

Commercial banks are one of several financial institutions that serve the economy. Others include thrifts (savings and loan associations and mutual savings banks), credit unions, investment companies, pension funds, insurance companies, and finance companies. An examination of their traditional roles helps an observer of the industry to appreciate the dramatic transformation that has taken place.

In the classification of *depository institutions* are *commercial banks, savings and loan associations, mutual savings banks,* and *credit unions.* That is, they all issue deposits--money that can be withdrawn upon demand or according to terms of the deposit agreement. For many years, these deposits formed the basis for the country's payments mechanism. That was before money took the form of electronic impulses rather than physical currency and coin.

Savings and loan associations (S&Ls) were originally established to provide real estate finance by accepting small savers' deposits and investing in residential mortgages. *Mutual savings banks* were also originally geared to the small investor. These institutions made mortgage loans and accepted primarily savings deposits. Like S&Ls and mutual savings banks, *credit unions* provide a savings vehicle for the small investor. They originally invested these funds in small consumer loans for purposes other than residential housing. Members of credit unions shared some form of common bond, frequently employment or occupation.

Other *nondepository institutions* include *investment companies, pension funds, insurance companies*, and *finance companies*. Traditionally, the financial instruments that they offered for sale to the public could not be used as money. But advances in technology have minimized this apparent limitation. *Investment companies* (for example, Fidelity mutual funds) pool money in small denominations to make large purchases of corporate and government securities. To this extent, they are similar to commercial banks, but investment companies issue ownership shares, not deposits, to their investors. The rate of return from an investment company share depends on the rate of return of the securities in which the company invests, with no guarantee or insurance for the investor.

Pension funds offer their investors deferred income. Contributors to pension funds receive the promise of lump-sum or periodic payments at or during retirement from employment. Contributions into pension funds are made by both employers and employees. Funds are invested in loans to industry and in securities issued by industrial firms.

Insurance companies promise protection from a variety of specified risks in exchange for investor funds. This promised protection is documented in an insurance policy. The two major types of insurance companies are life insurers and property and casualty insurers. Life insurers protect investors from death and disability during the term of the policy. (Some life insurance policies also include a savings component.) Property and casualty insurers protect against all other risks--automobile insurance is an example. Like pension funds, insurance companies invest policyholder funds in loans to and securities of commercial enterprises.

Finance companies offer services for both consumers and businesses. In one sense, they are similar to commercial banks, because they make loans. But finance companies generally make riskier loans than banks--that is, there is often a higher probability of non-repayment of loans that finance companies make. As a result, finance company loan rates have historically been higher than bank loan rates. Also, finance companies do not accept deposits, but issue securities similar to those of nonfinancial firms.

The Industry Transformation

In the past, these financial institutions tended to specialize. For example, commercial banks have been an important part of the economy's payments system and a major source of short-term finance for industry. Banks now offer consumer, real estate, and longer-term commercial services. Over time, many institutions diversified into other activities so that functions now frequently overlap, with the result that commercial banks are subject to increasingly intense competition.

Competition in financial services has blurred the difference between many formerly distinct institutions. For example, all depository institutions along with life insurance companies now provide mortgage finance. Also, all depository institutions, investment companies, and securities brokers and dealers offer accounts that are checking accounts for all intents and purposes. Investment companies offer rates of return to small investors that are often more attractive than rates available at depository institutions.

Changing Market Shares

The effect of the blurring of niches has been a decline in the importance of commercial banks and other depository institutions. In 1964, depository institutions had 58 percent of the total financial assets held by financial institutions. That share is now approximately 30 percent. The primary beneficiaries of this shift have been investment companies (mutual funds) and pension funds. The competitive rates of return available through investment companies have clearly attracted investors, particularly small investors, away from depository institutions. At the same time, the significant growth in assets under management at both investment companies and pension funds has given corporations alternatives to bank loans. Thus, banks face threats to both their deposit base and loan portfolio.

Particularly hard-hit, the U.S. savings and loan industry has shrunk from almost 4100 in 1960 to fewer than 1700 currently. The income on long-term, fixed-rate mortgage loans was insufficient to cover the cost of maintaining their deposit base as money market interest rates rose dramatically during the 1970s. During the 1980s the riskier investments that S&Ls were permitted only served to worsen the situation. The U.S. S&L industry severely contracted and probably will never resume its former importance as provider of mortgage finance.

For their part, banks have lost much of their low-cost deposits and top-tier corporate loan business. At the heart of this effect is a change in the interest rate environment that has produced a trend toward direct financing of corporate America. Major corporate clients have found it more economical to borrow short-term funds in the commercial paper market directly from the investing public rather than to borrow from a bank. Commercial paper allows large, creditworthy firms to borrow for periods of up to 270 days. The commercial paper rate has been only slightly higher than the Treasury bill rate (the lowest short-term rate available) since 1975, while the prime rate (charged to such large bank borrowers) has been significantly higher.

The amount of U.S. commercial paper outstanding represented less than 5 percent of the amount of domestic bank loans in the mid-1960s. This percentage has increased steadily, so that now commercial paper represents 40 percent of the dollar value of outstanding U.S. bank loans, a trend that has significantly contributed to a decline in commercial bank market share. Many industrial firms have replaced the commercial bank loan with commercial paper and long-term debt instruments such as bonds.

What has been lost in the business sector has been gained in the mortgage market. In the last 20 years, bank mortgage loans rew from 18 percent of all mortgages to 25 percent. Over the same period, consumer loans by banks have maintained a consistent market share in consumer finance.

Banks are important providers of finance in all three markets. Unfortunately, business loans have become increasingly competitive.

The New Global Banking Environment

The banking environment has indeed become more international. Since the early 1980s, U.S. banks have deemphasized growth in their international asset portfolios. There are several reasons for this. Third-world loan losses prompted many U.S. banks to withdraw from lending to developing countries. Also, U.S. banks divested of foreign affiliates in order to purchase domestic banks and failed depository institutions (savings and loan associations and other commercial banks). Lastly, the new capital standards of the Basle Accord made it necessary for money center banks to raise their capital ratios. Selling overseas affiliates serves this purpose because it reduces the amount of risk-weighted assets.

Citicorp is currently the most aggressive U.S. bank in terms of international operations. For example, the bank continues to increase its Asian personnel, targeting affluent Asians. The strategies and services of its Asian program include the following:

- In Asia, the name of Citibank is readily recognized as a high-quality provider of financial service. The bank capitalizes on this image.
- Each customer with a minimum $100,000 deposit has a personal banker.
- These clients are seen in a luxurious private office and served tea or coffee in fine China.
- Financial transactions can be conducted in eight different currencies.
- The same type of service is available to these clients when they travel to other countries.

This Asian program is considered highly profitable.

Foreign Bank Presence

While the U.S. banks that followed their corporate clients abroad in the 1960s and 1970s have withdrawn in many cases, banks from other countries that followed their clients to the United States have not retreated in the same manner. Also, the large size of the U.S. market has also been an attraction for foreign banks. The importance of the dollar in trade with the U.S. has also played a role in the expansion of foreign banks in the United States.

An interesting example of the cultural advantage that foreign banks sometimes enjoy in the United States can be seen in the area of Chinese banks. A few years ago, the Flushing area of Queens, New York had few Asian residents. Currently, more than 200,000 Chinese and Korean immigrants reside there. Asian banks are, likewise, an important element of the economy. The oldest Chinese-American bank in Flushing is Asia Bank. Others include Amerasia Bank and Hong Kong-Shanghai Banking Corporation.

One of the newest entrants is China Trust, one of the largest banks in Taiwan. In its first two weeks of operation, China Trust took in $6 million from 400 depositors. Of course, American banks compete aggressively for Asian deposits. For example, ATMs in Flushing offer transactions in three languages and the employees in Citibank's Asian Banking Center speak Korean, Mandarin, and Cantonese. Nevertheless, the Oriental banks have certain competitive advantages:

- Deposit interest rates are higher than at American banks.
- Weekend banking hours are maintained.
- In some cases, free parking (a rare commodity) is provided.
- The reputations and past records of customers from the home country are considered in credit evaluations.
- Gifts are often distributed during Chinese New Year.

The success of Asian banks in Flushing is not an accident. Competitive pricing, a high level of service, and cultural links all contribute.

In terms of location, foreign banks operating in the United States are concentrated in larger cities. Almost half are located in New York, with other large concentrations in Los Angeles, Chicago, Houston, and San Francisco. Representative offices and branches are the most common organizational form, followed by agencies.[1]

---

[1] There are four general forms of business organizations through which a bank may conduct overseas operations. The *representative office* is the most restricted of the four.

In terms of the markets that these banks serve, most are involved in corporate banking. This is also true of Japanese banks that serve more than 1,000 subsidiaries of Japanese industrial firms in California. In addition, these banks also cater to the large Japanese population in that state. They have also gained significant market share by offering banking services with thin profit margins. Bank acquisitions have helped increase their market share.

These banks do not act in isolation, however. For example, Bank of Tokyo-Mitsubishi Bank owns the Bank of California. With the help of Bank of Tokyo-Mitsubishi Bank (and Mitsubishi Trust and Tokio Marine and Fire Insurance companies), Mitsubishi companies have purchased a metal company, a power plant, and a mining concern in the state of California. Elsewhere in the United States, Mitsubishi financial companies have been involved in the acquisition or construction of a nonferrous smelting facility, a forklift operation, a chemical company, a glass manufacturer, a computer disk maker, a semiconductor- and wafer-fabricating facility, a big-screen television plant, and an options trading venture.

The current trend of Japanese banking in the United States is to seek more profitable transactions in the middle market, that is, medium-size corporations. Of course, this is the same corporate market that U.S. banks have targeted for future growth. This implies a trend of increasing competition between U.S. and Japanese banks in the United States.

Representative offices may *not* accept deposits, make loans, or conduct any banking services. They are simply points of contact between parent banks and their clients. *Agencies* have somewhat more authority. They may accept predetermined payments in connection with international trade or deliver undisbursed portions of loans made by the parent bank. However, deposit-taking or fiduciary activities (such as portfolio management) are strictly prohibited. Essentially, no credit decisions are made by agencies. Agencies may only execute credit decisions made by the parent. *Branches* and *subsidiaries* perform all normal banking functions. In the United States, a foreign *branch* must be licensed by either the state in which it is located or by the federal government. Technically, the results of operations are not distinguished from those of the parent bank. As a result, its lending limits are tied to the capital and surplus of the parent. Laws and regulations of the home country govern branch activities. *Subsidiaries* are separate legal entities, incorporated by the government of the country in which they operate. Each has its own capital base. However, it is not uncommon for the parent bank to own 100% of the subsidiary's stock. Generally, laws of the host country govern the operation of overseas subsidiaries. The choice of organizational form will depend upon a number of circumstances. If the bank has a large number of clients in the overseas location or a small number of major clients, a full service bank (branch or subsidiary) may be preferable. On the other hand, a representative office is a cost-effective way to explore a new geographical market before setting up more extensive operations.

The general focus on international banking is not limited to Japanese banks. This trend is changing the nature of commercial lending in the United States. Foreign banks now account for almost 50 percent of all commercial loans in the United States.[2] This situation is directly attributable to the retrenching of many U.S. banks from international operations. U.S. manufacturers turn increasingly to export markets for sales growth. The supply of export finance that is available through indigenous U.S. banks does not meet the increasing demand. Although exact figures are not available because the transactions involve proprietary information, it has been estimated that affiliates of foreign banks provide over half of the commercial trade finance in the United States. Often the vehicle used for this purpose is a letter of credit. Basic letter of credit transactions can be more easily carried out between branches of the same international bank--one in the exporting country, the other in the importing country.

In addition, industrial companies sometimes require financing of their continuing overseas operations that is difficult to obtain from U.S. banks. For example, Charles Machine Works, Inc., a manufacturer of construction equipment in the United States recently looked to establish a banking relationship to finance its inventory for its European dealers. The company has upwards of $200 million in annual sales, a solid balance sheet, and trenching-digging machine that has been included on *Fortune Magazine's* list of 100 products that America makes best. Charles Machine Works is an ideal example of a middle-market company with strong international growth potential. But because U.S. banks (which have traditionally served such companies) do not have meaningful overseas operations or connections, this company is forced to look for European banks--one country at a time--that will provide the necessary financing. Clearly, such industrial firms represent strong growth potential in U.S. commercial banking.

Conclusion

Traditional banking services can be obtained now from any number of financial institutions, including investment companies, insurance companies, and pension funds, and finance companies. Competition between domestic

---

[2] The earlier analyses referred to total loans, including, but not limited to, commercial loans.

and foreign institutions is becoming much keener. From a relatively small foreign presence less than three decades ago, international interests in the United States are now substantial. The economies of the world clearly are becoming more integrated. If anything is a constant in the changing financial services industry, it may be the continuing trend toward integration of institutions, markets, and economies. Commercial banks must rise to the challenge of international competitiveness.

Selected References

Barth, James R. R. Dan Brumbaugh, Jr., and Robert E. Litan. *Banking Industry in Turmoil: A Report on the Condition of the U.S. Banking Industry and the Bank Insurance Fund*, U.S. Government Printing Office, Washington, D.C., December 1990.

Board of Governors of the Federal Reserve System. *Flow of Funds Accounts; Financial Assets and Liabilities*, Washington, D.C.

Casey, Robert W. "Foreign Lenders Piling Up Gains in U.S.," *United States Banker*, April 1993, pp. 30-32,71.

Chandler, Clay. "Japanese Bid to Bail Out Banks Weighed Down By Conflicts, Concern About Using Public Funds," *Asian Wall Street Journal*, October 19, 1992.

Federal Deposit Insurance Corporation. *FDIC Quarterly Banking Profile*, Washington, D.C.

Hardy, Quentin. "Bank of Tokyo Unit to Buy 28 Branches of Bank America," *Asian Wall Street Journal*, March 9, 1992.

Holstein, William J., James Treece, Stan Crock, and Larry Armstrong. "Hands Across America: The Rise of Mitsubishi," *Business Week*, September 24, 1990, pp. 102-107.

Krarr, Louis. "How Americans Win in Asia," *Fortune*, vol. 124, no.8 (October 7, 1991), p. 140.

Leung, Julia. "Bank of America Unveils Asia Plan in Wake of Merger," *Asian Wall Street Journal*, April 27, 1992.

Leung, Julia. "U.S. Banks Are Poised for Further Expansion In Asia This Year As Demand for Services Grows," *Asian Wall Street Journal*, February 24, 1992.

Liner, Doug. "Some Trends in Export Financing," *Export Today*, May 1993, pp. 39-41.

Lorch, Donatella, "Banks Follow Immigrants to Flushing," *New York Times*, August 7, 1991. pp. B1-B2.

Task Force on the International Competitiveness of U.S. Financial Institutions. *Report of the Subcommittee on Financial Institutions Supervision, Regulation, and Insurance*, U.S. Government Printing Office, Washington, D.C., October 1990.

U.S. Department of Commerce, Bureau of Economic Analysis. *Business Statistics*, Washington, D.C., various issues.

U.S. Department of Commerce, Bureau of Economic Analysis. *Survey of Current Business*, Washington, D.C., various issues.

2. International Variations

Introduction

Commercial banks in all industrialized countries share certain common features. Each banking system is involved in the payments mechanism, in the provision of consumer services, and in financial support of industrial firms. There are differences, however, in the form of these services and the extent to which the pace of technological change has transformed the services themselves. U.S. banks are generally smaller than their counterparts in other countries and frequently have a more narrow scope of bank powers. At the same time, U.S. banks are pushing the frontier of permitted services and developing technology-based financial specialties.

Banking in an International Context

Of the world's 1000 largest commercial banks in 1999, 40 percent were in Europe, 18 percent in North America, and 27 percent in Asia, with the rest of the world accounting for 15 percent. Together, the top 1000 banks control assets of roughly $35 trillion. The banking systems of the United States, Canada, the United Kingdom, Germany, France, Switzerland, and Japan control a large share of the world's banking assets.

The United States

Unlike banking systems in other countries, the United States has a large number of both state-chartered and national commercial banks. The number peaked at 30,000 in 1920 but because of failures and mergers is less than 10,000. Twenty-eight percent of these are nationally chartered, hold almost 60% of U.S. bank assets, and control 53% of U.S. bank offices. Thus, national banks are large with ample branch networks. In terms of number of separate banks, however, the largest group is non-Federal Reserve member state institutions representing about 60% of all commercial bank charters. These smaller institutions represent only 18% of bank assets and 31% of bank offices. The smallest group in terms of number of charters, Federal Reserve member state banks, hold roughly 11% of bank charters, but 18% of assets and 16% of offices.

As a result, national banks have average total assets of about $1.1 billion, state-chartered Federal Reserve member banks $1.2 billion, and non-Fed member state-chartered banks $160 million. Across all banks, the average size is $548.5 million. While New York is often described as the U.S. money center because the country's largest banks are headquartered there, the structure of the U.S. banking system is essentially a diverse collection of institutions with limited geographical service areas. Among industrialized countries, the United States is unusual in this regard. Even when regional banks operate in other countries, a strong system of banks that branch nationwide is the rule rather than the exception.

The United Kingdom

Prior to 1914, London was recognized as the world's center for international finance. The pound sterling was the major currency of the world because London has historically provided significant amounts of long-term investment capital and short-term trade finance. Furthermore, the government of the United Kingdom has a long tradition of facilitating domestic and international trade.

For centuries, the Bank of England--a private bank with certain government privileges--oversaw all banking operations and monetary policy. After being nationalized in 1946, the Bank received the power to give directives to other banks, a power that it did not exercise. Instead, its quasi-official status and its ability to affect the liquidity of other commercial banks, just as the Federal Reserve does in the United States, made it possible for the Bank of England to achieve its desired results through requests. In general, the banking system of the United Kingdom is based on convention and mutual understanding between government, the Bank of England, and other institutions.

Clearing banks in the United Kingdom perform the same functions as commercial banks in the United States. In particular, clearing banks provide the nation's primary payments mechanism (checks and other forms of payment) and short-term liquidity to industrial firms through extensive overdrafts.[3] Unlike U.S. banks, British clearing banks branch nationwide. This system has resulted in a relatively small number of clearing banks that process 80% of all check and credit card transactions. Among these, the largest are:

- HSBC Holdings
- Barclays Bank
- National Westminster Bank
- Lloyds TSB Bank

Secondary banks, also known as *merchant banks*, offer primarily time, rather than demand, deposits. Competition among secondary banks is aggressive and the banks use interest rates to attract large, wholesale deposits. To match the average maturity of deposits and loans, secondary banks generally make longer-term loans, frequently to non-British enterprises.

Both clearing and merchant banks use discount houses to adjust their liquidity levels. Discount houses are intermediaries between the government and the clearing banks. These private firms absorb the entire weekly U.K. Treasury Bill offering, can borrow from the Bank of England, are active dealers in short-term government securities, and make a secondary market with merchant banks in negotiable CDs and acceptances. The Bank of England does not make direct loans to nor conduct open market operations with banks, as the Federal Reserve does in the United States. Instead, the Bank of England conducts these transactions with discount houses; in turn, the discount houses deal directly with the banks.

Canada

The Canadian banking system is a blend of the U.S. and U.K. systems. Structurally, it resembles the U.K. system in that banks branch nationwide, but its monetary policy implementation is similar to that of the United States with the Canadian central bank having direct relations with the commercial banks.

The Bank of Montreal, the first true bank, began operations in 1817 and received a charter in 1822. The bank's charter contained provisions that illustrate the strong governmental influence over Canadian banks. The

[3] An overdraft is a check written for which there are insufficient bank funds that the bank honors, effectively granting the check writer a short-term loan.

original charter was granted for only 10 years, prohibited the bank from owning real estate other than bank promises and from making loans collateralized by real estate, required annual reports to shareholders with specified information, and placed a ceiling of 6% on loan interest rates. In the United States, in contrast, strict government supervision of commercial banks did not begin until enactment of the National Bank Act of 1863.

The Finance Ministry of Canada implements both fiscal and monetary policy. The original Bank Act was passed in 1871 and subsequent amendments to the act have shaped the financial system over time. The Bank Act amendment of 1924 established the Office of the Inspector General of Banks, Canada's the primary bank examiner. The Canadian central bank, the Bank of Canada, was created by a 1934 amendment to the Bank Act.

Restrictions of bank operations have eased over time. Residential mortgage loans with a 15% government guarantee have been permitted since 1936. In the mid-1940s, the government began to guarantee short- and intermediate-term bank loans to farmers and veterans. Also, the government lifted loan interest rate ceilings in 1967 (13 years before the major deregulatory thrust in the United States), allowed banks to offer discount brokerage services in the early 1980s, and permitted banks to own securities firms in the late 1980s (a practice permitted for only a few commercial banks in the United States).

Generally, there has been a good relationship between government and the banking industry. Canadian banks have been permitted to expand lending powers as desired and have enjoyed virtually complete freedom to offer a variety of deposits. This contrasts with the U.S. experience in which expansion of banking powers has been permitted primarily by bank regulators rather than by legislators because of the reluctance of legislators to pass further bank liberalization laws.

The Canadian equivalent of commercial banks is *chartered banks*. Between 1820 and 1970, 157 charters were granted. Sixty of these, however, were never used, 45 banks either failed or ceased operation for some other reason, and there were a number of bank mergers. These factors have caused the number of Canadian banks to be much smaller than the number of U.S. banks. Five chartered banks control roughly 90% of Canadian bank assets:

- The Royal Bank of Canada
- The Canadian Imperial Bank of Commerce

- ScotiaBank
- The Bank of Montreal
- The Toronto-Dominion Bank

These five operate branching networks throughout Canada, a practice only recently permitted for U.S. banks.

Germany

Commercial banks in the Germany have even greater operational freedom than Canadian banks. Past abuses of power by the government have resulted in a general disdain for government intervention in the banking system.[4]

Moreover, individual states in Germany have a long history of regional strength and independence from the central government, resulting in several cities with significant economic influence. Bonn and Berlin are the political centers; Hamburg is the busiest port and second largest city; Dusseldorf is a major manufacturing site; and Frankfort is the financial center. In this respect, German banking is comparable to U.S. banking, with a large number of state and regional banks.

In contrast to the U.S. system, however, the Deutsche Bundesbank, the German central bank, does not restrict the scope of bank activities. German banks offer corporate underwriting services and hold the common stock of their clients as investments. Because of this wide range of bank services, German banks are called *universal* banks. The central bank does, however, perform customary roles of lender of last resort and facilitator of monetary policy. The German banking system has operated in this way since shortly after the end of World War II.

In addition to the state and regional banks, there are three big banks in Germany:

- Deutsche Bank
- Dresdner Bank
- Commerzbank

With assets of over $1.4 trillion, these three banks control half of all German bank assets and branches and, like Canadian banks, operate nationwide.

---

[4] Germany suffered hyperinflation after World War I and, again, during World War II as a result of the abandonment of sound central banking principles by the Reichbank (central bank prior to creation of the Bundesbank). Extensive credit created for use by the German government severely devalued the country's currency and destabilized the entire economy.

France

Before World War I, Paris was second only to London as an international financial center. Although France was ravaged by both World Wars, Paris has since regained much of its former status in world finance. In 1945, the four largest deposit banks were nationalized and all banks were required to assume one of three forms: *banque de dépôts* or deposit bank (accepting deposits and granting loans), *banque d'affaires* or investment bank (granting loans and taking equity positions), or *banque de crédit à long et moyen terme* or medium- to long-term credit bank. Deposit banks receive demand deposits or any deposits repayable within two years. Business banks underwrite new securities issues. Medium- to long-term credit banks offer loans and accept time deposits that have a longer term than the deposit bank instruments. Subsequently, the remaining deposit banks were also nationalized.[5]

In 1966, however, the distinction between deposit banks and business banks was weakened in a move toward bank deregulation. In 1984, the distinctions were completely eliminated when the *établissement de crédit* and its functions replaced the former three categories of institutions. Currently, French deposit banks offer a full line of financial services, including short- and medium-term loans, demand and time deposits, and securities dealing and underwriting.

Like Germany, France has a number of large banks that dominate the industry. The largest French banks are:

- Banque Nationale de Paris
- Societé Générale
- Paribas
- Crédit Lyonnais
- Banque Indosuez
- Credit Commercial de France

Switzerland

Swiss commercial banks operate in an environment of privacy that is unmatched in the rest of the world. The 1934 Banking Law, the first federal banking law in that country, contained provisions that protected depositors in

---

5. In 1986, Société Générale was returned to private ownership among companies that were friendly to the French government.

Swiss banks. Banks are prohibited from revealing details of financial transactions to outsiders unless an illegal act, according to Swiss law, is involved. This secrecy provision was partially motivated by attempts of agents of Nazi Germany to determine the nature and amount of Swiss deposits owned by German citizens. The bank secrecy law protected private citizens from the misguided whims of government by allowing depositors to use accounts identified with numbers only, the so-called "numbered accounts," and by preventing transactions disclosure.

The provisions of the 1934 Act have, nevertheless, created some tensions between the governments of Switzerland and other countries. Tax evasion and insider stock trading, for example, are considered criminal acts in the United States, but are prosecuted administratively (in civil proceedings) in Switzerland. Because they are civil offenses in Switzerland, these acts do not override the bank secrecy law. In the interest of good international relations, however, the Swiss government has cooperated with the United States in some cases involving insider trading violations. Along these same lines, beginning in 1991, the actual owner of all Swiss bank accounts, not a lawyer or other agent for the depositor, must be known by at least two bank officials.

Switzerland has had a favorable financial climate for other reasons. The Swiss people themselves have long been ardent savers, with the result that the country has consistently been a net exporter of capital. Consistent with its respect for privacy, Switzerland has remained politically neutral, avoiding burdensome expenses of war. Stability of the Swiss franc and the Swiss banking system after World War I contributed to its reputation of a safe haven for funds. As a result, during the 1920s and 1930s, the country's commercial banks received large deposits, primarily from Germany.

Over time, Switzerland's economic stability, political neutrality, and bank secrecy law have attracted capital worldwide. Foreign banks have likewise been attracted to Switzerland's stable financial markets.

Liechtenstein is a sovereign state approximately one hour's drive from Zurich and shares its currency, legal structure, and customs with Switzerland. Because of these shared characteristics, Liechtenstein has also become involved in the world of international banking.

Like German banks, the major banks in Switzerland are also universal banks. The five largest institutions control almost 50% of all Swiss bank assets. The two largest are:

- UBS

- Crédit Suisse Group

(In 1998, Union Bank of Switzerland merged with Swiss Bank Corporation and changed its name to UBS.) Swiss banks are heavily involved in capital markets and equity investments in industrial firms.

Cantonal banks are publicly owned and restricted to the geographical areas in which they are located. While these 29 institutions are considered banks, they tend to specialize in savings deposits and mortgage loans but also offer financial services to local industry. Controlling roughly one quarter of bank assets, cantonal banks are the second most important group of banks.

Foreign banks represent the third largest presence in Switzerland, greater than domestic savings banks and credit cooperatives. With over 100 foreign institutions, Switzerland is one of the world's largest international financial centers.

Japan

The 1868 Meiji Restoration was an early turning point in the economic development of Japan, replacing the prior feudal system that had generated little economic progress for the country. The Meiji government established the Osaka Mint in 1871 and passed the New Currency Act. The 1872 National Bank Act established national banks, similar to those in the United States. The objectives of these acts were to create a stable currency and to mobilize funds for needed development. Although there were 153 national banks by 1879, the individual savings rate was quite low, most loans were agricultural, and there was limited availability of small business loans.

Rapid expansion of the money supply through the new national banks led to widespread inflation in 1877 through 1880. In turn, the inflation necessitated an amendment of the National Bank Act that created Japan's central bank to facilitate industrial finance, lower interest rates, and increase the resources available to financial institutions. The Bank of Japan began operations in 1882 and was given sole note-issuing power after 1899. All other banks were reorganized as ordinary banks.

The ordinary bank classification is composed of *city banks* and *regional banks*. City banks are large, nationwide organizations that target major industrial firms, while regional banks cater to the needs of smaller businesses and individuals. The activities of regional banks are typically limited to one prefecture or state.

Prior to World War II, Japanese banks were often members of large industrial combinations called *zaibatsu*. Through this mechanism, strong ties between banks and industrial firms were formed with the largest *zaibatsu* banks, Sumitomo, Mitsui, and Mitsubishi being particularly instrumental in Japan's economic development.

After World War II, *zaibatsu* were dismantled and *keiretsu*, or industrial groups with interlocking ownership, formed. Former zaibatsu banks still provided the majority of debt financing to their *keiretsu* affiliates. Although the regional banks channeled their savings deposits to the *keiretsu* city banks through interbank loans, until the 1970s city banks were consistently overloaned. Overlending is the situation in which a bank's loan demand consistently exceeds available deposits and capital.

The Bank of Japan relieved the overlending by making loans to the city banks. The Bank of Japan encouraged loans to high priority industries by offering its loans to city banks at favorable interest rates, which were then reflected in favorable interest rates to industrial firms. Overlending ended after the 1970s when Japan became a net capital exporter because of large trade surpluses. While industrial firms are now less dependent on their *keiretsu* banks, they still maintain close relationships.

In the late 1920s, there were approximately 1,000 ordinary banks in Japan. During World War II, many were liquidated or consolidated so that by 1945, only 61 ordinary banks remained. Today, 9 city banks hold roughly three quarters of total bank assets:

- Bank of Tokyo-Mitsubishi
- Sakura Bank (formerly Mitsui Bank and Taiyo Kobe Bank)
- Fuji Bank
- Sanwa Bank
- Dai-Ichi Kangyo Bank
- Sumitomo Bank
- Tokai Bank
- Asahi Bank
- Daiwa Bank

The Structural Differences

Average Size

Even with a large share of total banking assets, U.S. banks often operate at a competitive disadvantage because their average size is so much smaller. Consider the following breakdown of average bank size for these countries in 1994.

	# of banks	Average Assets ($ billions)
United States	10,489	$ 0.38
United Kingdom	37	30.49
Canada	11	46.92
Germany	273	4.53
France	421	2.85
Switzerland	230	2.92
Japan	140	49.33

The average size of U.S. banks is much smaller than the average in the other countries shown. This significant size difference is important because a growing share of banks operating in the United States are foreign banks and compete directly with U.S. domestic banks. To the extent that U.S. banks are smaller and less able to offer a full range of services, domestic banks will continue to lose market share on their own turf.[6]

The size difference is important also because industrial firms operate increasingly in a global environment. The future international competitiveness of the United States will depend in large measure on the ability of small- and medium-size firms to sell their goods and services abroad. Just as the large *zaibatsu* banks helped Japanese industrial firms to compete and to expand internationally, so too U.S. banks can assist U.S. firms. However, this assistance might be limited by the size of the bank because a smaller bank's loan portfolio can more easily become overly

---

[6] See Chapter 1 for a description of the increasing trend of foreign bank loans as a percentage of total bank loans in the United States.

concentrated in one industry. Furthermore, it is not certain that foreign banks will have the same kind of commitment to U.S. firms that U.S. banks have.

Population per Bank

The relative small size of U.S. banks is not tied to the lack of banking assets in this country, but to the large number of banks. The number of banks in the United States is much greater than the other countries analyzed. Admittedly, the populations of these countries are smaller than the U.S. population--but not so much as to reconcile the difference in number of banks. The population per bank in the United States in 1994 was is 25,000 people. This statistic indicates a relatively high number of banks--one bank for every 25,000 residents. Switzerland had the next smallest population per bank at 30,000. The United Kingdom had the highest such statistic--1.568 million residents per bank or 63 times the U.S. statistic.

Availability of banking services has not necessarily been compromised by the smaller number of banks in other countries. The population per bank branch among the six countries noted above is remarkably similar. In the United States, France, the United Kingdom, and Switzerland, the population per bank branch is between 4,500 and 6,000 people. In Japan and Germany, the number is no more than twice this level. Thus, the convenience and availability of banking services need not be compromised in a banking system of larger institutions.

Comparative Bank Services

Payment Mechanisms

Checks in the United States

Historically, *checks* have been the second most preferred method of payment in the Unites States, with *cash* representing the greatest number of transactions—as much as 70 percent of all transactions. Yet in terms of dollar volume, checks represent a much larger amount of payments.

Individuals write the greatest number of checks in the United States. The payees of these checks are primarily businesses, with governments and other individuals receiving less than 10% of them. The next most frequent check writers are businesses, making payments to other businesses, to individuals, and to governments. Governmental bodies write less than 10% of checks.

To clear these checks, banks rely on check-clearing systems. The system can either be a local clearing house or a Federal Reserve clearing system if the banks are not in the same area. In the United States, Fedwire is operated by the Federal Reserve and is the official network for clearing domestic checks. This system is also used for market transactions between the Treasury Department and the Federal Reserve.

With the volume of checks that is processed each day, financial transactions would be delayed considerably if each bank waited to determine its overall cash position before paying those checks drawn on it. The net result of this clearing activity is that total interbank deposit accounts (those accounts that banks have with other banks) can be as much as $100 billion out of balance. These temporary imbalances necessitate borrowing in short-term money markets such as overnight loans (called federal funds) and repurchase agreements (involving Treasury and other marketable securities).

Many of these money market transactions are recorded on bank-owned electronic networks. Clearinghouse Interbank Payments System, or CHIPS, processes large payments between banks and even banks and their clients. Bankwire, a smaller bank-owned network typically gets the overflow from Fedwire and CHIPS.

In the past, some payee banks placed holds on checks until they cleared payor banks. If the payees were not advised of these "holds," they could write checks that exceeded their *available balance*, that is, that portion of the account balance that may be withdrawn immediately. In some cases, banks would not pay interest on the deposit until the end of the predetermined "hold period," even if the deposited check cleared before that time.

To correct these problems, Congress passed the Expedited Funds Availability Act of 1987. The act did not prohibit holds because banks have a legitimate need to protect themselves against check fraud or forgery. Instead, the law set a maximum hold period on specific accounts. The law states when interest on the deposit must begin accruing and requires that the bank tell its customers when funds will be available.

Not all accounts are covered by the legislation. Only transaction accounts are subject to the law. This includes demand deposits and N.O.W. (negotiable order of withdrawal) accounts. No holds may be placed on U.S. Treasury checks or U.S. Postal Service money orders. For other checks, the hold period depends on whether payee and payor banks are in the same Federal Reserve check-processing zone. If they are in the same zone, the maximum hold is one business day. If they are not, the maximum is four business days. The Federal Reserve is responsible for implementing this law. Federal Reserve regulation CC is the enforcement regulation.

Notwithstanding the time limits imposed by Regulation CC, it can take 6 to 10 days for an out-of-town check go through the system and the advice be returned to the payee bank. If such a check was drawn on an account with insufficient funds, the payee bank would have already released the funds to its customer. This possibility has encouraged the development of more efficient clearing systems.

An example of a more efficient clearing system is Electronic Check Presentment or ECP. The basic principle underlying ECP is that the information on a check may be shared electronically much faster than the physical check can be shipped. The bank in which a check is deposited scans the magnetic ink character recognition (MICR) line. This information is wired to the bank upon which the check is drawn. If there are insufficient funds for the check, the check is flagged overnight instead of a week later.

ECP standards and practices in the United States are being developed through the Electronic Check Clearing House Organization (ECCHO) with member banks including Citibank, Bank of America, and Chase Manhattan. The procedure is being tested in the states of Michigan and California. More than 1,000 banks currently have the computer capacity to receive some sort of electronic check information.

While there are obvious benefits, the cost of ECP is also substantial. A bank that wishes to send checks electronically must invest $50,000 and applicable training costs. A bank that wishes to receive checks electronically should expect to invest an additional $200,000 to $300,000. However, the availability of such timely information can be turned into a fee-generating operation. For example, a corporate bank customer that has deposited a check for goods can be advised if the check will not be honored before any merchandise is shipped. Also, ECP can eliminate many of the delays associated with check processing for small, remote banks that have correspondent relationships with large banks. Part of the cost of ECP systems can be deferred by charging fees for the advance information that the system generates. In any event, as ECP applications become more common, the cost will undoubtedly decline.

Check Writing in Other Countries

The check-writing habit is also well developed in Canada, but the clearing function is much different. Five major banks control the vast majority of total bank assets. Reciprocal agreements among them have all but eliminated payor float, that is, the time that elapses between the payee's receipt of a check and the corresponding reduction in the payor's account. Consumer checks are paid on a same-day basis, despite the fact that actual settlement occurs the next day. Writers of checks in denominations of $50,000 or more (business transactions) are assessed any float costs that accrue. Of course, this system is possible because there is a high degree of concentration in the Canadian banking system. In addition, nationwide branching of the five major banks has resulted in distributed locations and comparable market share.

In Europe, most countries have a *giro system* that performs the function of checking accounts in the U.S. A giro system is a nonbank payments system (frequently at the post office) that transfers funds from one account to another on a same-day basis. Because payments are effected at a centralized location, there is no payor float. The bank transaction in the United States that is most similar to a giro transfer is an "on-us" check, that is a check deposited in the same bank on which it is drawn.

Interestingly, the giro system of the United Kingdom is not used as frequently as its continental European counterparts. This is partially because the U.K. Post Office Giro system was not introduced until 1968. More fundamentally, however, British clearing banks have long emphasized personal banking services, branching nationwide and encouraging the use of checks. The major U.K. clearing banks dominate the retail banking market, controlling the majority of all personal bank accounts.

In contrast, in Japan, checks and giro transactions originate almost exclusively in the business sector. Japanese payments are much more frequently in the form of cash or electronic transfer. The Japanese postal savings system has no parallel in the United States. The system accumulates savings from individuals and small businesses. It is a popular outlet for savings because the interest income was tax-exempt for deposits up to ¥3 million until 1988 and because there are over 20,000 locations, compared to approximately 10,000 bank branches. Currently, accounts may be maintained with balances up to ¥5 million. While interest income on these accounts is no longer tax-exempt, the interest rate is attractive as compared to other alternatives. Also, the postal system is extremely convenient. Through the postal savings system, wire transfers are easily done. Transfers are possible not only to all domestic locations, but also to almost 100 other countries that have agreements between their postal authorities and Japan's.

Automation has clearly affected the payment mechanisms. The impact of automation on payments exceeds beyond check clearing and cash transfers, however.

Credit Cards in the United States and Abroad

As compared to cash and checks, credit cards are a relatively new means of payment that has become extremely popular. The first cards were introduced in the 1950s, at which time, card payees manually telephoned to receive authorization for each transaction. The current technology uses plastic cards with magnetic stripes on the back. The magnetic stripe enables payees to verify cards electronically before accepting them as payment. This verification is via a communications network set up over telephone lines. Credit cards are convenient and reduce the need to carry cash. Because card verification is now so streamlined, many retail establishments frequently accept credit cards more readily than checks.

For banks, credit cards are a profitable product line because income is realized in several ways. In every case, the payee accepting the credit card for payment does not receive the full amount shown on the *credit card draft*, that is, the sales slip created in a credit card transaction, showing amount, payee, payor, credit card issuer, and payor signature. The draft is an instruction by the payor to the credit card issuer to pay the amount shown to the payee. However, when the draft is presented to the credit card issuer, it is discounted by 3 to 5 percent. The *discount* is a source of income for commercial banks that issue credit cards.

If the bank charges an *annual fee* to cardholders (usually $25 to $50), these fees are also income for the bank. The payor receives a monthly statement from the bank that lists the transactions for that month. Typically, if the cardholder pays the bank for these transactions before the specified due date, no interest is charged. If not, the bank earns *interest income* on unpaid balances. The interest rate on credit cards loans is higher than other forms of consumer lending, often in excess of 18%. Because of this high rate, the discounts, and annual fees, credit card operations can be quite profitable. Of course, there is also a relatively higher probability of uncollectible loans since most credit cards are unsecured.

Credit card business is concentrated among the largest banks in the United States. Originally, Citicorp began card operations in New York state, subject to a 12 percent usury law loan rate ceiling. Subsequently, the state of South Dakota relaxed entry requirements for bank holding companies and eliminated interest rate ceilings. Citicorp transferred all of its credit card operations to a bank in Sioux Falls where loans and receivables are subject to no interest rate ceilings. This strategic move is but one of many innovative techniques that Citicorp, the largest bank holding company in the United States, has employed to maintain a competitive advantage with respect to retail banking.

In addition, Citicorp has designed private label credit cards for retail merchandisers such as Goodyear and Tandy Radio Shack. A private label credit card program is one in which a financial institution manages the credit card operation of a retailer, including promotion, credit evaluations, billing, and accounting--all in the retailer's name.

The credit card networks of Visa and MasterCard have introduced innovations in an effort to differentiate themselves. For example, Visa has a "procurement card" that can be used for small corporate purchases under $5000. The card incorporates internal controls that limit the type and amount of purchases for which the user can receive authorization. In addition, the corporate card owner can take advantage of flexible billing arrangements, including centralized billing procedures and reporting at multiple levels.

MasterCard offers a very upscale version of the gold card. Members of Louis Rukeyser's Wall Street Club, 400,000 investors who subscribe to his newsletter, may sign up for lines of credit up to $25,000 and a low initial interest rate. In addition, the cardholder is entitled to discounts on stock brokerage services, stock research, and quotations. The card will be closely watched by others in the industry as the first experiment in an affinity card that is linked with a high-profile personality.

Because of the healthy spread (difference between cost of funds and loan rate) that typically is available through credit cards, commercial banks face vigorous competition from outside their industry. Retailers such as Sears and even AT&T, the telecommunications giant, have credit cards that compete directly with bank-issued cards. But finance companies represent perhaps the strongest competing industry with many services that are directly comparable to those offered by commercial banks. For example, General Electric Capital Corporation (GECC) owns a credit card bank called Monogram Bank USA. A U.S. credit card bank is not subject to the same regulatory constraints as a commercial bank because it is designated to conduct primarily credit card business. GECC has issued over 35 million private label credit cards for major retailers such as the Macy's department store chain. Banks will no doubt continue to face mounting competition in this lucrative segment of the U.S. system of payments.

Travel and entertainment cards have been available in Europe for some time. However, bank credit cards are a recent innovation. With widespread acceptance and issuance of bank cards in the United States, American banks have turned to Europe for possible market expansion. In Germany, where bankers rely heavily upon their clients' presence in bank offices to cross-sell a number of products, the bank credit card received a cool reception.

To the displeasure of German banks, American Express purchased a Frankfurt bank through which insurance and other services were sold via credit card. Attempts to block this activity with regulatory intervention and with agreements among German banks for nonparticipation in the card venture proved unsuccessful. Unable to stop the introduction of the bank card, German banks joined with their own version, the Eurocard. In 1987, retailers announced plans to issue their own cards. The introduction of credit cards by American firms has facilitated market expansion. As a result, German residents now enjoy a broader range of financial services.

In the United Kingdom, the Barclaycard was the first. In some ways, the innovative spirit of Barclays is similar to that of Citicorp. Barclays is also the largest of Britain's clearing banks, with 5,000 branches worldwide.

In general, consumer banking services have been slower to evolve in Japan than in the United States or the United Kingdom. This is primarily because the larger city banks have historically focused on large corporate clients. The regional banks that did cater to individuals had neither comparable nationwide networks nor management. However, at the urging of the Ministry of Finance and certain political factions, city banks began to issue credit cards in the 1960s. The Japan Credit Bureau (JCB) is the most widely distributed.

The Union Credit card, the second most popular, is also jointly operated by Fuji, Dai-Ichi Kangyo, Saitama, and Sakura. Sumitomo, Mitsubishi, and Tokai have each independently marketed their own credit cards. As consumer credit is developed in Japan, credit cards and related services should be considered a growth industry in that country.

It should be noted that there may still be considerable payor float involved with credit card transactions. In this case, the float is the time necessary to process, invoice, and collect the sales drafts. In essence, card-issuing banks are compensated for this sometimes considerable float through the discount.

Telecommunications technology has enhanced the use of bank credits as a part of the payments system in the United States and abroad. In a similar way, the use of direct electronic payments has increased.

Electronic Payments

Electronic payments may take several forms. The *automated clearing house (ACH)* is similar to the European giro system in that both account balances change on the same day, with no payor float. In an ACH, a written agreement documents the transactions that will be covered by the service in which one party is entitled to initiate a transaction with another party. With one or two days notice to the bank, a given transaction is effected with hard-copy detail of the transaction following. The most common examples are payroll direct deposit, U.S. government payments, and recurring payments such as insurance premiums. The Federal Reserve processes most ACH transactions in the United States.

These transfers were the first electronic link between banks, an indirect connection. Large volume, regular payments are recorded by a bank for its customer (for example, a utility company) on a magnetic tape. The clearing house computer simply sorts the transactions on the tape, creating a new separate tape for each bank on the other side of the transfers. Output tapes are then used to adjust interbank balances.

Wire transfers eliminate the need for magnetic tapes and are more direct electronic links. Through Fedwire (Federal Reserve), CHIPS (Clearing House Interbank Payment, New York), SWIFT (Society for Worldwide Interbank Financial Telecommunications), or Cashwire (international, regional, and national private sector firms), large interbank transactions are settled on a same-day basis. Wire transfers are an extension of the special handling for important transactions such as money market purchases or sales. Currently, immediately available funds can be transferred to any other party almost instantaneously. The volume of interbank transfers on such networks, including check clearing activities, can easily amount to $2 trillion in a single day.

Point of sale (POS) electronic links theoretically accomplish the same objective as wire transfers. However, while wire transfers typically involve large denominations, POS is geared to the smaller high volume retail market, for example, grocery stores and service stations. In this context, *convenience* and *cost* are important considerations.

In order to be convenient, a standardized system with adequate distribution is necessary. Standardization may be achieved with plastic *debit cards* with magnetic strips contain information about the payor's account. Use of a debit card results in reduction of the payor's bank account balance, that is, a "debit" to the deposit account of that payor. The offsetting "credit" is to the payee's deposit account, or, alternatively, to the deposit account of the payee's bank. Telecommunications equipment that connects the records of participating banks makes it possible to simultaneously reduce the account balance of the payor by the amount of the retail transaction and increase the balance of the retailer.

Cost considerations are both in terms of out-of-pocket expense and security. Required hardware and software development can entail substantial initial investment. These fixed expenditures require a high volume of transactions to bring per-unit cost within a reasonable range. However, high volume will at least partially depend on public acceptance of this means of payment. From the consumers' perspective, the greatest benefit is the reduced need to carry cash. Yet checking accounts serve virtually the same function. Switching from checks to debit cards requires that consumers relinquish payor float. So, unless participating banks can price POS services in such a way that they are competitive with checks, the immediate advantages for consumers are not clear.

Aside from out-of-pocket expense, banks participating in the on-line arrangement described above must open their records to access by a system over which they do not exercise complete control. The more secure alternative of off-line transactions (perhaps through ACH) increases the probability of loss through use of invalid cards. The considerations of cost and security can be significant deterrents in the implementation of POS technology.

Cash dispensers (CDs) were the first applications of automation in retail banking. These early machines usually dispensed a fixed amount of currency in a single denomination and most were off-line. Fairly rapid advances have made it possible to receive larger amounts of currency and to perform other functions, such as loan payments, deposits, transfers between accounts owned by the customer, and payments to third parties. The later generations are referred to as *automated teller machines (ATMs).*

Some ATMs are positioned in an outside wall of the bank building to provide 24-hour access to bank services. Others are located in the lobby of the bank or in separate, adjoining lobbies. The enclosed ATMs provide greater customer security while using an ATM. Increasingly, ATMs are on-line operations, particularly in the United States.

Shared ATMs away from bank branches enable several banks to establish a "branch" in high density areas such as factories, hospitals, universities, and airports. Generally, banks have been reluctant to share ATMs on their own premises. Banks in various geographical regions have agreed to such arrangements in order to provide convenient service for traveling customers.

ATMs have been well received both in the United States and abroad. Full-service machines tend to be more common in the United States. However, universally, customers use ATMs primarily as cash dispensers often in connection with a credit or debit card.

In general, on-line debit cards have not been marketed as aggressively as credit cards which are generally considered more profitable. In this regard, commercial banks are not fully capitalizing on the portion of the payments system that still remains almost entirely within the banking industry--the debit card system.

In most cases, customer fees are based on actual transactions using the card. However, there is growing sentiment that the availability of the debit card itself should generate revenue for the issuing bank, just as in the case of credit cards. Before such charges become industry norm it will probably be necessary to increase the perceived value of the card. For example, the technology currently exists to increase withdrawal limits for customers with high checking account balances. Also, prestige card holders can be offered insurance protection or buyer protection plans that are now only associated with credit cards. Only a few brokerage firms have issued Visa Debit cards that give consumers access to their mutual fund accounts.

The field remains wide open for commercial banks to develop with relatively little competition.

Smart Cards

Smart cards are the next generation of alternatives to cash and checks. The computer chip in a smart card can validate a user's personal identification number (PIN), authorize retail purchases, verify account balances, and store personal records. The chip memory can also hold information on the user's relationship with, for example, a bank, a securities firm, or an insurance company. Each time the card is used, the personal data base is updated.

Technically, a smart card contains a computer chip instead of a magnetic strip. However, the first generation of smart cards were *prepaid* cards with magnetic strips, also called *electronic purses* or *stored-value* cards. The two most common uses of such prepaid cards have been prepaid transit cards and prepaid telephone cards. Transit authorities in New York City and Washington, D.C. use these smart cards to eliminate the use of tokens and to charge different fares for different routes. Telephone cards, representing a $1 billion in U.S. sales in the mid-1990s, are issued by MCI, AT&T, and GTE.

From the perspective of financial institutions, smart cards with magnetic strips represent less of a shift in technology than smart cards with computer chips. Retailers with whom the banks cooperate in POS facilities have invested heavily in magnetic strip technology. Examples of these retailers include oil companies (service stations), national food chains, and national department store chains. A move to chip cards will represent significant costs for a large-scale transition.

Another issue for financial institutions and the development of smart card technology is Regulation E (Reg E), the Federal Reserve regulation that sets rules, liabilities, and procedures for electronic funds transfers (EFT). Reg E also establishes consumer protections in EFTs. One of these protections is that receipts are generally required to document EFTs. This provision must be addressed before smart cards can be used to, for example, transfer funds between bank and securities accounts or settle insurance claims.

Lastly, the financial services industry must address the issue of consumer acceptance of smart cards. In the mid-1990s, few U.S. residents had been presented the opportunity to use a smart card. Thus, the level of consumer acceptance in the United States remained uncertain.

Check Truncation

The U.S. Federal Reserve has long been a champion of further efficiencies in the payments system, actively encouraging *truncation*--the ultimate efficiency in check processing. Truncation is a service in which canceled checks are held by the payor's bank or by another bank in the check clearing process, rather than being returned in the account statement. Checks can either be truncated at the bank of first deposit or by a Federal Reserve bank. Excluding canceled checks from customer statements saves the payor bank at least $1 per account per month. Given the thousands of accounts maintained by most banks, the savings can be substantial.

Under the electronic check clearing program of the Federal Reserve--available in all 12 Federal Reserve Bank districts--paper checks may follow the electronic exchange of payment data. However, if the bank requests, the Federal Reserve Bank will not forward the paper checks, but instead record microfilm copies or other images of the checks for later access by banks or their customers.

Imaging Technology

Employing *imaging technology* in check clearing means that a bank would receive graphical images of the checks drawn against it instead of the actual paper check. In the context of check clearing, imaging is the creation and transmission of an electronic picture (image) of a check during the check clearing process instead of shipping the physical check. The Federal Reserve also has much interest in this technology because it can provide backup support for truncating. Using images can assist the payor bank in such areas as pay-or-no-pay decisions and signature verifications.[7]

The biggest technical challenge in imaging the check clearing process is the correct interpretation of the written check amounts. *Character amount recognition* or *character amount read (CAR)* means that personnel need not manually read the numerals written in the courtesy amount boxes of checks. The challenge is that there are as many as 30 different ways that checks are written. The problems with CAR tend to center around three factors:

- The condition or readability of the physical checks.

---

[7] Such systems have been developed by technology companies such as IBM, Unisys, NCR, and Banctec Systems.

- The various ways that customers write checks.
- The variety of locations for the courtesy amount box on the checks.

Imaging technology significantly improves the work environment in the check processing work area. Typically, in this fast-paced operational area, two people who want to speak to each other must shout to be heard. With imaging technology, the same people may whisper and still hear each other. At the same time, the speed of processing has dramatically increases over conventional systems. An average, conventional check-clearing operation can clear about 1,400 checks per hour. An imaging system clears more than 20,000 per hour.

Expanding Technology

It is safe to say that banks now compete in large measure based on their technological edge. This extends beyond credit or debit cards to marketing services to customers and managing customer information. If the loan system does not communicate with the deposit system, for example, valuable customer-profile information can be lost. If systems procedures in various departments are significantly different, customers can get the impression that they are working with several different banks.

A solution to this problem is the use of client/server technology. The server is designed to be the host system or central system. The client refers to the user--a bank employee. The server manages the functions for the entire organization. It can be mainframe, a minicomputer, or a larger personal computer (PC). Each user performs his or her own proprietary functions, usually on a PC. This arrangement has gained popularity because it gives each user greater control over data and the computing process.

Whichever approach is taken, however, the trend is toward better management of technology. The basic steps to realizing the full benefit from technology are:

- *Defining what the bank wants to achieve with its technology*. Systems will have the two general components of (1) operation or transactions processing and (2) management information analysis, such as asset/liability information. The exact combination of these two component will depend on the system. The bank should decide which proportions are appropriate for its applications.

- *Identifying the bank's existing technology.* In some cases, hardware or software that the bank already owns could increase efficiency if it were fully utilized.
- *Integrating the technology.* If transactions information and management information technology are integrated, it is possible to identify customer profiles, analyze client segment profitability, and to produce better data for asset/liability management.

With the increased use of computer-based products, such as credit, debit, and stored-value cards, the bank that is to remain competitive must keep abreast of the developments in the field of bank technology.

Corporate Services

In the past, U.S. commercial banks fostered relationships with corporate clients such that one bank provided a number of services for a given firm. Loan pricing was a function of all the other services and their respective profitability. More recently, however, surplus corporate cash is more frequently invested in money market instruments, instead of bank deposits. Corporate loan pricing must now be competitive with commercial paper rates for large, creditworthy clients. Thus, performance and profitability measurement of individual services is critical.

Because of the diversity of clients, corporate services are often custom-tailored. In fact, banks engage in corporate banking to varying degrees. While Citicorp management places heavy emphasis on retail banking, other money center banks have tended to specialize in corporate accounts. J.P. Morgan, the holding company of Morgan Guaranty, is an example of this. Morgan Guaranty's management has shaped the organization into a wholesale operation, with only 2% of the New York Metropolitan area branches of Citibank. The holding company also owns, partially or completely, subsidiaries engaged in trust, real estate, investment, international, and merchant banking activities.

The Shrinking Top-Tier Corporate Clientele

Whatever the degree of emphasis on corporate services, certain trends are undeniable. Historically, commercial banks have earned substantial spreads by assuming credit risk of their corporate clients and financing these loans with relatively inexpensive deposit funds (demand or savings deposits). The cost of deposit funds has become more volatile since the 1980s. Further, larger corporations more frequently use commercial paper financing at more favorable interest rates. Thus, traditional spreads are no longer available on loans to major corporations.

During the early 1990s, low short-term interest rates made investments in long-term government securities extremely attractive for commercial banks. Also, the Basle Accord capital guidelines have encouraged investment in government securities by placing a zero risk-weight on this category. This means that there is no capital requirement for these instruments. On the other hand, commercial and industrial loans are assigned a 100 percent risk-weight, that is, must be backed by a full 8 percent of capital. The effect of market forces and regulatory requirements is reflected in changes in bank portfolios in 1992. Commercial and industrial loans decreased by $22.5 billion to $536.3 billion--a 4 percent decline. During the same year, securities portfolios grew by $81.4 billion to $772.8 billion--a 12 percent increase.

One consequence of this situation is that small- and medium-sized firms represent a market segment with significant future growth potential. Because these corporations have relatively less access to money and capital markets, they must necessarily depend more heavily upon commercial banks and other financial intermediaries. To cultivate a new client in this category, it may be necessary to employ direct mail, telemarketing, calling officers, seminars, or special events. This can be a relatively expensive process (perhaps as much as 300 basis points) if the resulting loan or deposit balance is in the $50,000 to $100,000 range—as can easily be the case for a smaller firm. Also, smaller firms are more likely to fail within two to three years, preventing the bank from recovering the cost of account acquisition through interest and fees.

Nevertheless, the market is large, with more than 10 million small businesses in the United States alone. In a recent survey by the Bank of Montreal, it was shown that 80 percent small businesses have only one account with a given bank and 60 percent have an account with more than one bank. At the same time, the most profitable small business clients maintain multiple relationships with a given bank. The key to enhancing bank profitability in the middle market is to integrate information about existing clients and to provide them with a wider range of bank services.

Emphasis on Fee Income

Another consequence of the thinner spreads available on loans to larger corporate customers is that fee income has become a much more important part of bank profitability. Thus, conventional services such as checking accounts and associated activities (e.g., stop payment orders and items returned for insufficient funds) are now important fee income generators.

However, there are some fee-generating segments that are not being exploited. Letters of credit for U.S. exporters is one of these. Unfortunately, U.S. banks are losing ground to U.S. offices of foreign banks that are more willing and, in some cases, able to provide this form of trade finance. Sometimes foreign banks have an advantage because they may be knowledgeable about their home markets or have long-time relationships in specific areas of the world. In addition, other foreign banks specialize in dealing with public and privately supplied export credit insurance for use on short-term exports of less than $100,000 or in selling foreign trade receivables.

Nevertheless, a U.S. bank can generate fees at several levels in assisting exporters with letters of credit (L/Cs). Consider a transaction in which a U.S. exporter requests an L/C from the foreign buyer. When the L/C from the overseas bank is sent to the United States, it is received by a U.S. bank that acts as an *advising* bank, that is, the bank that assures the authenticity of the L/C. The advising fee is generally $50 to $150. If the U.S. bank agrees to *confirm* the L/C, that is, to guarantee payment (even if the foreign bank does not pay), the fee is 12.5 to 300 basis points based on the amount of the L/C. Finally, when the merchandise has been shipped, the L/C is *negotiated*, that is, the exporter is paid. This generates another 12.5 to 50 basis points based on the amount of the L/C. Thus, a U.S. bank that advises, confirms, and negotiates a $100,000 L/C can realize as much as $3,650 in fee income ($150 + (.035 x 100,000)).

In addition to traditional lines of business, commercial banks have begun to offer other services many of which produce fee income.

- foreign exchange and treasury services
- data processing
- highly leveraged loans
- a greater volume of commercial real estate loans
- off-balance-sheet commitments

Multinational clients with domestic and international telecommunications networks can contract with the bank for worldwide cash flow information. With the assistance of the bank, receipts and disbursements can be more readily offset, often reducing the required number of foreign currency transactions. The bank performs all the required transactions, sometimes including risk management techniques that compensate for the multinationals' total exposure in specific currencies. To the extent that bank cash management techniques and technology are more advanced than those of its client, the client is more likely to contract with its bank.

Smaller corporate clients will not usually require such assistance. Instead, payroll or general ledger maintenance may be an appealing and appropriate service. This arrangement generally involves little or no incremental cost for the bank but enables it to sell unused time on its computer system. Since the bank already has cash flow details in connection with its clients' deposit and loan accounts, it has a comparative advantage over other data processing services.

Securities Operations

Other possible fee income generators remain at least partially off-limits for U.S. commercial banks. Since 1933, when the Banking Act (Glass-Steagall) was passed by Congress, U.S. banks have been restricted with respect to investment banking activities. The Act required that commercial banks divest themselves of investment banking affiliates. No national bank or state bank that was a member of the Federal Reserve could *directly* deal in, underwrite, or purchase securities. Furthermore, no entity engaged in the business of issuing, underwriting, selling, or distributing securities could accept deposits. While Glass-Steagall *did* permit national banks to buy and sell securities without recourse as agents for their customers, subsequent rulings by the U.S. Comptroller of the Currency prohibited commercial banks from engaging in brokerage activities.

Until recently, most securities activities continued to be off-limits. Exceptions to this general rule were transactions involving fixed-income, investment-grade securities, such as federal government securities and general obligations of state and local governments. Glass-Steagall allowed national banks to own, deal in, and underwrite these instruments in U.S. markets and to engage in private placements.

Full-scale underwriting activities by U.S. banks are permitted in overseas markets. The net result of this regulatory difference is that only those banks that are large enough to maintain substantial overseas operations have been able to enter the securities business to any meaningful extent. At least in this respect, small- to medium-sized banks have found themselves at a competitive disadvantage as compared to larger institutions.

While U.S. commercial banks are not permitted to engage in securities underwriting in the United States, foreign banks have long been permitted to do so. This is because, before 1978, foreign banks operating in the United States were not subject to Glass-Steagall. The *International Banking Act of 1978* had the effect of prohibiting foreign banks from engaging in securities underwriting. However, 17 foreign banks were grandfathered, that is, permitted to continue to operate existing securities affiliates in the United States. Among these, there are eight German firms, three French, three Swiss, and one Japanese. Of course, the ability of these firms to do securities underwriting places domestic firms at a competitive disadvantage.

Federal legislators have thus far not been responsive to these apparent competitive inequities. While recent banking laws have served to remove interest rate ceilings and to provide for more attractive deposit instruments (e.g., N.O.W. accounts, small-saver certificates and money market deposit accounts), they have *not* relaxed prohibitions against securities operations. In 1991, the Secretary of the Treasury Department proposed, among other things, that commercial banks in sound financial condition, be permitted to engage in securities transactions through a separate affiliate. To date, there has been no Congressional action on this recommendation.

In the absence of legislative measures, U.S. bank regulators have granted expanded powers with respect to securities activities. During the 1980s, the Federal Reserve Board and the Comptroller of the Currency permitted bank holding companies and national banks to:

- Underwrite commercial paper, mortgage-backed securities, municipal revenue bonds, and consumer-related receivables through subsidiaries that underwrite U.S. government securities.
- Place commercial paper without recourse for the account of customers.
- Transfer the commercial paper to a holding company subsidiary.
- Issue, underwrite, and deal in collateralized mortgage obligations through finance subsidiaries.

- Offer securities brokerage and investment advisory services to institutions.
- Offer and sell units in a unit investment trust solely on the order and for the account of the bank's customer through a bank or bank holding company subsidiary.
- Make limited investments in an investment bank.
- Create and sell interests in a publicly offered common trust fund for individual retirement account assets.

Beginning in 1987, the Federal Reserve interpreted the Glass-Steagall Act in such a way as to permit banks to engage *indirectly* in securities activities. Section 20 of the Glass-Steagall Act prohibits Federal Reserve member banks from affiliating with any organization "engaged principally" in the issue, flotation, underwriting, public sale, or distribution of securities. (Other provisions of the Act prohibit a bank from participating in these activities *directly*.) The Federal Reserve interpreted Section 20 as permitting a bank to affiliate with a firm engaged in securities transactions as long as securities transactions are not the principal business of the firm.

The Federal Reserve gave bank holding companies the right to establish nonbank subsidiaries that earn up to 10% (later increased to 25%) of revenue from otherwise prohibited securities transactions. These transactions include underwriting of and dealing in:

- commercial paper
- mortgage-backed securities
- municipal revenue bonds
- securitized assets
- corporate bonds
- corporate equities

To ensure that the affiliation with banks is truly indirect, "firewalls" must be constructed and maintained. These firewalls limit transactions between the Section 20 subsidiary and the bank so as to limit risk to the bank, limit bank subsidies to the Section 20 sub, and prevent conflicts of interest between the two.

Generally speaking, commercial banks are moving more toward securities transactions for their own accounts as well as for clients, especially the larger banks. Typically, regional banks are less involved in trading activities because of the potential volatility in earnings. Recently, investment funds to make it possible for all banks to participate in securities trading are appearing. For example, Farrell Capital Management (FCM) has operated since 1988 with this objective. The primary fund is Globe Map I for which FCM is the registered investment advisor. This is a new area for many smaller banks, but one that promises to grow as banks become more involved in securities transactions.

The U.S. securities industry has challenged these developments, but these attempts have generally been unsuccessful. It is more likely that Congress will validate these powers and further expand the scope of banking activities. While it is not likely that U.S. bank powers will expand to this extent, the German banking system presents an interesting case of commercial bank involvement in industrial finance.

While U.S. banks attempt to provide a wider range of fee-generating services to corporate clients in order to bolster profitability, German banks have long enjoyed a much broader scope of corporate activity. German banks underwrite corporate securities and hold large portfolios of stock. As long as a German bank is adequately capitalized, there is virtually no regulatory limit on equity investments or other involvement in nonbank corporations.

In addition to their own equity positions, German banks are major depositories for individual shareholders. These individuals may authorize their depository bank to vote their shares during annual shareholder meetings. Because most agree with their bank's policy position with respect to a given industrial firm, bank influence over the corporate sector is even further enhanced.

Thus, it is common for bank representatives to hold seats on corporate boards of directors. Since German banks (1) hold significant shares in their own accounts, (2) represent most of the votes of shares deposited with them, and (3) provide the bulk of debt finance to industry, corporations also seek bank financial advisory service. Firms generally have a "house bank" that exercises significant influence over managerial decision making.

The house bank has close day-to-day contact with its corporate client, not simply as a cash manager or arms-length third party, but as an industry specialist, a readily accessible research facility, and a confidant. While French and Japanese banks also have close working relationships with their corporate clients, the German model is, perhaps, the <u>best</u> example of the extent to which bank/industry relations can be developed to facilitate industrial development. In contrast, in the United States relationships have not been permitted to evolve to this extent.

In 1983, the Federal Reserve Board permitted BankAmerica Corporation to purchase Charles Schwab Corporation. Since then more than 2,000 banks and bank holding companies in the U.S. have begun to offer discount brokerage services.

During the early 1980s, stock market participation by individual investors increased significantly, largely because of strong, broadly based stock price increases. The Dow Jones Industrial Average (an index of 30 blue-chip stocks in the United States) rose from 836 at the end of 1979 to 2,225 in October 1987, or at an average rate of 13% per year. During the same period, the annual inflation rate (as measured by changes in the consumer price index) averaged 5%. The 8% average real rate of return (13%-5%) available in the early and mid-1980s lured many individual investors into the stock market. The subsequent stock market crash in October 1987 discouraged many individuals and caused this segment of the market to contract. But in the meantime, discount brokerage firms grew faster than more traditional, full-service brokers. This phenomenon is also due to demographic factors. As the "baby boom" generation (born shortly after World War II) ages, its members have more time to analyze their investments, that is, will be less dependent on the *advice* of brokers. For these investors, convenient, low-cost transactions are an appealing alternative.

Beyond demographic considerations, individual investors are becoming more sophisticated with respect to investment opportunities. A consequence of this heightened awareness is interest rate and price sensitivity. This sensitivity helps to account for the growth in interest-sensitive bank deposits and the discount brokerage business.

Within the discount brokerage industry, bank brokerages appear to have enjoyed particularly strong growth. One of the most popular vehicles has been the fixed annuity contract. These are rather straightforward, tax-deferred investments that are typically offered through an insurance company. With the current low level of interest rates, these contracts have lost much of their appeal, however. A more recent trend is the sale of variable annuities, also available from insurance companies, that perform more like mutual funds. In fact, the variable annuity is a combination of a mutual fund and an annuity. The attractions of a variable annuity over a mutual fund are tax-deferral and guarantee of principal. The bank earns a commission on the sale from the issuing insurance company. Some banks that offer proprietary mutual funds, contract with insurance companies to wrap the insurance protection around the mutual fund and create the equivalent of a variable annuity. In either case, the variable annuity market is considered a strong candidate for future growth in the banking industry.[8]

In general, commercial banks possess certain comparative advantages in the discount brokerage business. The name recognition of the bank is a strong marketing tool in that *confidence* in the brokerage firm is easier to establish. Also, bank clients are already familiar with the institution making it possible to incur less *advertising* expense. Lastly, existing bank customers are ideal *prospects* for brokerage services. Thus, while nonbank discounters have had to rely on television and newspaper advertising, bank brokerages have been able to successfully use less costly advertising such as direct mail and bank statement enclosures.

The securities industries, both corporate services and retail brokerage, have substantial growth potential for commercial banks. As the conventional intermediation functions of accepting deposits and making loans continue to be challenged by nonbank competition and shrinking spreads, banks will seek these and other avenues to diversify their product mix. The insurance industry also holds promise.

Insurance

When the office of the U.S. Treasury Secretary recommended in 1991 that well-capitalized banks be permitted to engage in securities activities, it was also proposed that full-service insurance activities be permitted. The National Bank Act (1863) permits national banks to engage only in underwriting and brokerage of insurance that is incidental to banking. This includes credit life, accident and health insurance. The Bank Holding Company Act (1956) and the Garn-St Germain Act (1982) prohibit bank holding companies (companies that own banks) from engaging in <u>any</u> insurance activity. However, existing insurance operations were grandfathered when the legislation was passed. Also, national banks and

---

[8] In the United States, in order to offer variable annuity contracts, the seller must have a Series 6 (permitting sales of mutual funds) or Series 7 (permitting sales of stocks and bonds) securities license as well as a current life insurance license for the applicable state. In some states, a specific variable annuity license may be required. In contrast, sellers of fixed annuity contracts need only a life insurance license.

bank holding companies in towns of fewer than 5,000 persons are exempted from the prohibitions.

The banking industry has long taken the position that banks should be allowed a more active role in the insurance industry. Arguably, insurance is quite similar to banking in that:

- Banks accept deposits; insurance companies accept premiums.
- Both types of institutions invest the money in order to generate a profit.
- Eventually both depositors and policyholders are repaid.

If a bank were permitted to perform these functions in the insurance industry it would be an *insurance underwriter*, that is, the company that assumes full responsibility of paying the benefits promised in an insurance policy.

Because insurance underwriting can give rise to large liabilities associated with benefit payments, the U.S. Treasury recommended that any bank-run insurance operations be confined to a separate insurance affiliate and that "firewalls" be constructed around the bank. This is similar to the Treasury recommendation for a separate securities affiliate for those banks on sound financial footing. A separate affiliate with bank firewalls limit risk to the bank.

Even if a bank does not engage in full underwriting activities, a bank-run *insurance agency* can increase noninterest income significantly. An insurance agency is a company that sells insurance policies for an insurance underwriter. Since the insurance underwriter bears the ultimate burden of paying insurance claims, the commissions earned by an insurance agent are also riskless income. Also, banks could provide cost-effective "packages" of:

- mortgage loans and mortgage insurance (insurance that repays the mortgage in the event of death or disability of borrower)
- auto loans and auto insurance
- small business loans and "key individual" insurance (insurance that covers those people who are most important to the operations of the business)
- corporate loans and corporate life or property/casualty insurance (insurance that covers all employees and property of the corporation)

As is true in the case of securities operations, U.S. federal regulators have attempted to liberalize national bank powers. The Office of the Comptroller of the Currency (which charters national banks) has given permission to national banks to underwrite and sell title insurance (protecting the buyer of real estate property from ownership claims of previous owners) and property insurance related to loan collateral. National banks have also been granted the right to broker fixed-rate annuities (insurance policies that pay a stream of fixed payments rather than a lump-sum).

Federal regulators have attempted to liberalize bank powers within the framework of existing federal law that relates to national banks, state banks that are members of the Federal Reserve, and banking holding companies. Only U.S. Congressional action can change the federal law. Meanwhile, state-chartered banks that are not members of the Federal Reserve are not subject to many of these existing laws. More than half of all bank charters belong to state-chartered nonmembers. The expansion of bank powers is much more pronounced within this group.

Conclusion

Commercial banks are an integral part of the economy in all industrialized countries. In the United States, commercial banks serve a relatively small geographic area because nationwide branching is not permitted. In other major trading partners of the United States, there is no such prohibition. One of the consequences of this is that U.S. banks are on average much smaller than banks in other industrialized countries. Furthermore, the large trade surpluses of Japan have led to that country's banks dominating the ranks of the world's largest. The competitive position of U.S. banks will improve, however, as the number of banks is reduced through consolidation and nationwide branching is instituted.

Universal functions of commercial banks are accepting deposits and making loans. In most cases, these deposits represent a significant part of a country's money supply. However, technological advances have led to changes in both the delivering and form of payments services. Credit cards and the use of ATMs now frequently substitute for check-writing. Point-of-sale facilities are also operational. Commercial banks can maintain part of their competitive advantage in the payments system by introducing wider uses for debit and stored-value cards.

Greater access to money and capital markets by large corporate bank clients has meant thinner margins in corporate lending activities. As a result, banks have turned increasingly to fee-generating services and to the middle segment of the corporate market. Cash management, data processing, commercial paper underwriting, and provision of discount brokerage facilities are some of the services being emphasized.

Selected References

The Top 1000 World Banks, Special Issue of The Banker, July 1999.

Bank Profitability, Statistical Supplement, Financial Statements of Banks 1994, Organization for Economic Co-operation and Development, Paris, 1996.

Bayliss, B. T. and A. A. S. Butt Philip. *Capital Markets and Industrial Investment in Germany and France; Lessons for the U.K.*, Saxon House, Westmead, England, 1980.

Bean, Randall. "Banks' Big Opportunities in Small Business," *Bankers Monthly*, January 1993, pp. 35-36.

Beckwith, Burnham P. "Eight Forecasts for U.S. Banking," *The Futurist*, vol. 23, no.2 (March-April 1989), pp. 27-33.

Boreham, Gordon F. "Canadian and U.S. Banking Systems: Some Comparisons," *Canadian Banker*, vol. 94, no. 3 (1987), pp. 6-14.

Borowsky, Mark. "Banks Are Betting On Electronic Presentment," *Bank Management*, April 1993, pp. 26-28.

Bronte, Stephen. *Japanese France: Markets and Institutions*, Germany Publications, London, 1982.

Coler, Mark and Ellis Ratner. *Financial Services; Insiders' Views of the Future*, New York Institute of Finance, New York, 1988.

Compton, Eric N. *The New World of Commercial Banking*, Lexington Books, Lexington, Massachusetts, 1987.

Davies, Michael S. "Exploiting Opportunities in Small-Business Lending," *Journal of Retail Banking*, vol 15, no. 1 (Spring 1993), pp. 33-37.

Federal Deposit Insurance Corporation. "Quarterly Banking Profile," various issues.

Federal Deposit Insurance Corporation. *FDIC Statistics on Banking*, Author, Washington, D.C., various issues.

Gart, Alan. *Banks, Thrifts, and Insurance Companies; Surviving the 1980s*, Lexington Books, Lexington, Massachusetts, 1985.

Giesen, Lauri. "Debit Cards Get Some Respect--Finally," *Bank Management*, January 1993, pp. 47-51.

Gillis, M. Arthur. "Unscrambling the Jargon: A Glossary of Terms in the Technology Arena," *Independent Banker*, vol. 43, no.4 (April 1993), pp. 26-27.

Grady, John, and Martin Weale. *British Banking 1960-85*, St. Martin's Press, New York.

Hay, Tony. *A Guide to European Financial Centres*, St James Press, Chicago, 1990.

Horne, James. *Japan's Financial Markets*, George Allen and Unwin North Sydney, Australia, 1985.

International Financial Statistics, International Monetary Fund, Washington, D.C., Yearbook 1990.

King, Mary L. *The Great American Snafu*, Lexington Books, Lexington, Massachusetts, 1985.

Kurtzman, Joel. *The Death of Money: How the Electronic Economy Has Destabilized the World's Markets and Created Financial Chaos*, Simon & Schuster, New York, 1993.

Lawrence, Colin and Robert P. Shay. *Technological Innovation, Regulations, and the Monetary Economy,* Ballinger Publishing Company, Cambridge, Massachusetts, 1986.

Lees, Francis A. and Maximo Eng. *International Financial Markets: Development of the Present System and Future Prospects*, Praeger Publishers, New York, 1975.

Liner, Doug. "Some Trends in Export Financing," *Export Today*, May 1993, pp. 39-41.

Marshall, Jeffrey. "Variable Annuities: Hope or Hype?" *United States Banker,* June 1993, pp. 25-26.

McRae, Hamish and Frances Cairncross. Capital City; *London as a Financial Centre*, Methuen, London, 1984.

Milligan, John W. "Who's Afraid of Proprietary Trading?" *United States Banker*, July 1993, pp. 12-14.

Mitchell, Richard and Robert Kazel. "Finding New Uses for Debit Cards," *Bank Management*, January 1993, pp. 52-55.

Mullineux, Andrew. *International Banking and Financial Systems: a Comparison,* Graham and Trotman, London, 1987.

Mullineux, A. W. *U.K. Banking After Deregulation*, Croom Helm, London, 1987.

Neufeld, E. P. *The Financial System of Canada,* Macmillan Company of Canada, Toronto, Canada, 1972.

Pecchioli, R. M. *Prudential Supervision in Banking*, Organisation for Economic Cooperation and Development, Paris, 1987.

Pressnell, L.S. *Money and Banking in Japan*, St. Martin's Press, New York, 1973.

Radigan, Joseph. "Can Branch Automation Deliver the Goods?" *United States Banker*, May 1993, pp. 65-67.

Rehberg, Virginia J. "Letters of Credit: Cracking the Code," *Export Today*, September 1991, pp. 21-23.

Revell, J. R. S. *Banking and Electronic Fund Transfers*, Organization for Economic Cooperation and Development, Paris, 1983.

Revell, Jack. *The British Financial System*, Macmillan Press, Ltd., London, 1973.

Rosenbluth, Frances McCall. *Financial Politics in Contemporary Japan*, Cornell University, Ithaca, New York, 1989.

Skully, Michael T. *Financial Institutions and Markets in the Far East; A Study of China, Hong Kong, Japan, South Korea, and Taiwan*, St. Martin's Press, New York, 1982.

Spong, Kenneth. *Banking Regulation; Its Purposes, Implementation, and Effects*, 3e, Federal Reserve Bank of Kansas City, 1990.

Subcommittee on Financial Institutions Supervision, Regulation and Insurance. *Report of the Task Force on the International Competitiveness of U.S. Financial Institutions*, Committee on Banking, Finance and Urban Affairs, U.S. House of Representatives, Washington, D.C., 1991.

Suzuki, Yoshio. *The Japanese Financial System*, Oxford University Press, New York, 1987.

Suzuki, Yoshio. *Money and Banking in Contemporary Japan*, Yale University Press, London, 1980.

U.S. Department of the Treasury. *Modernizing the Financial System; Recommendations for Safer, More Competitive Banks*, Washington, D.C., 1991.

Viner, Aron. *Inside Japanese Financial Markets*, Dow Jones-Irwin, Homewood, Illinois, 1988.

"Visa's Corporate Card Push," *United States Banker*, August 1993, pp. 46-47.

"Wall Street Cache," *United States Banker*, August 1993, p. 47.

Weiner, Jerry. "Your Technology: It May Be Better Than You Think," *Independent Banker*, vol. 43, no. 4 (April 1993), pp. 24-25.

Wilson, J. S. G. *Banking Policy and Structure: A Comparative Analysis*, Croom Helm, London, 1986.

3. Driving Forces of Change

Introduction

The financial markets of the world are evolving into high-technology networks over which billions of dollars, marks, yen, and francs are traded each day. The forces that are driving this evolution include the development of offshore financial markets that are subject to little, if any, regulation; the move toward deregulation within national boundaries; and the creation of a harmonized financial system within Europe.

Euromarkets, where home-currency instruments are traded outside national borders, provide alternative financing vehicles and investment opportunities. Eurocurrencies, particularly Eurodollars, have proved effective in correcting international liquidity imbalances for banks, industrial firms, and sovereign governments. Eurocurrency markets that started in London are now found in other European cities, and in Singapore, Hong Kong, Tokyo, the Cayman Islands, and the Bahamas, while London is still the site of most Eurobond issues and active secondary trading. Eurocommercial paper, Euronotes, and Euroequities have all grown rapidly.

Within national boundaries, limits on the scope of activities of depository institutions in the presence of volatile interest rates threatened the continued existence of many financial institutions in the United States. Movements toward deregulation have put in motion a force that will forever change the nature of commercial banking in the United States and other countries. The 15-nation European Community continues to move toward a full integration of the markets for goods and services, including financial services. The Single European Market represents a landmark event in the growth of cross-border financial investments.

Euromarkets

Euromarkets are financial markets that involve instruments either denominated in a currency that is not the local domestic currency, or denominated in the domestic currency but sold in non-domestic markets, or distributed by a international syndicate of investment bankers or merchant banks. This is a comprehensive definition that describes a multitude of financial instruments and arrangements. These activities can be found in four general market classifications:

- Currency markets
- Bond markets
- Commercial paper markets
- Equity markets

Currency Markets

Eurodollars form the core of international money markets transactions. Eurodollars are deposits denominated in U.S. dollars issued by banks outside the U.S. Even if the bank's home office is in the U.S., the deposit is considered a Eurodollar deposit. These markets developed as the result of a number of factors.

In the late 1950s and 1960s, banks in Western Europe, the Middle East, the Far East, and elsewhere began actively to trade U.S. dollars for reasons having to do with international trade and U.S. legislation.

In 1957, Great Britain severely restricted non-British borrowing and lending in British pounds. At about the same time, countries in Western Europe liberalized bank trading in U.S. dollars to facilitate formation of the European Common Market.

During the 1960s, U.S. exports of goods and services exceeded imports by $40 billion, which created a net international demand for dollars to pay for the American goods. The supply of dollars came primarily from capital outflows of $52 billion from the United States for large investments in foreign capital assets as U.S. firms established international operations.

These large holdings abroad of U.S. dollars (still convertible into gold) and the accompanying conversions strained the nation's gold reserves and shook international faith in the soundness of dollar. The U.S. government reacted with several pieces of legislation to restrict capital outflows. The *Interest Equalization Tax (IET)* of 1964 discouraged the issuance of foreign securities in the United States by effectively increasing by 1% the cost of financing for foreigners. When evidence showed that the IET merely encouraged more bank financing, bank loans were subsequently included in IET provisions.

The *Voluntary Foreign Credit Restraint Program (VFCRP)* of 1965 recommended limitation of the amount of foreign lending and investment by commercial banks, insurance companies, and pension funds. The program also asked industrial firms to improve their individual capital flows either by exporting more goods and services, by postponing marginal foreign direct investment, or by raising more funds abroad.

The 1968 *Foreign Direct Investment Program (FDIP)* placed mandatory restrictions on direct investment to advanced European economies, Australia, and South Africa. More liberal ceilings applied to developing countries.

The net effect of these regulations was to put pressure on the multinational customers of U.S. commercial banks to fund their foreign operations outside U.S. markets. Moreover, loan rates that banks could offer foreign borrowers were not as competitive as they would have been otherwise. U.S. industrial firms found it difficult to turn to their domestic banks for financing and foreign borrowers found significant disincentives to borrow from U.S. banks. These factors combined to significantly reduce demand for bank loans in the United States.

At the same time, U.S. commercial banks were subject to Regulation Q (Reg Q) of the Federal Reserve, which placed ceilings on deposit interest rates. When, in 1966, Reg Q ceilings for negotiable certificates of deposit (NCDs) were below market rates, banks responded by offering more competitive NCD rates in their foreign offices, offices in which they were not subject to Req Q. The overseas NCDs, known as *Eurodollar CDs*, became a significant source of funds for U.S. commercial banks, especially because they were not subject to costly reserve requirements and deposit insurance premiums.

Investment of the proceeds from Eurodollar CD sales was, likewise, not subject to the IET, VFCRP, or the FDIP. Thus, Eurodollars provided banks with liquidity to finance the foreign operations of U.S. multinational firms. Even after the Reg Q ceiling on domestic NCDs was removed in 1970 and the capital outflow legislation was abolished in 1974, the Eurodollar market continued to flourish, primarily because of the absence of reserve requirements and deposit insurance premiums.

London became the most important Eurodollar financial center because of its long tradition as an international financial center with well-developed money, interbank, and discount markets. Equally important is the absence of strict regulations with respect to foreign currency transactions by non-British financial institutions. As a result, banks from other countries have been able to establish a virtually unregulated presence in London.

Paris is the second largest Eurodollar market, although its transactions volume is much less than that of London. Frankfurt, Amsterdam, Zurich, Basel, Geneva, Milan, and Vienna also maintain Eurodollar operations. The Cayman Islands and the Bahamas have become major Eurodollar markets primarily because of tax advantages.

Since 1968, when the withholding tax on interest payments made to nonresidents was removed, Singapore has been an important center for U.S. dollar deposits. Both Hong Kong and Tokyo are now also designated *Asiandollar* financial centers. Singapore has generally dominated Hong Kong and Tokyo, because its tax environment has been the most favorable and foreign exchange controls have been almost nonexistent. Dollar deposits even in Asia are frequently referred to as Eurodollar deposits. In fact, the "Euro" designation applies to any transaction made outside the home country of the currency involved.[9]

Currency traders are often located in one large room at a bank, where each trader has access to several telephones, video screens, and news tapes. A trader generally specializes in one or a small number of currencies, communicating with other traders at banks around the world. Interbank transactions are in wholesale denominations of $1 million or more. An unusually large currency exchange may be facilitated by a broker working on a commission basis with several banks. Long-standing relationships and preestablished lines of credit allow both sides of a trade to make firm commitments over the telephone.

The currency markets operate 24 hours a day in different time zones around the world. When the New York market closes at 5 p.m., the San Francisco market is still open. At 8 p.m., New York time, the San Francisco market closes, and the Tokyo market opens. An hour later (9 p.m., New York time), the Hong Kong and Singapore markets open. At 3 a.m., Tokyo closes but Frankfurt opens. An hour later (4 a.m., New York time), Hong Kong and Singapore close, and London opens. This continuous operation

[9] The use of the term "Euro" is not connected with the single currency of the same name.

and almost instantaneous, firm commitments via telephone make the foreign currency markets the most efficient in the world.

The volume of trading in currency markets is more than $1 trillion per day. Historically, most of this trading was controlled by banks. More recently, however, fund managers have become important participants in currency market trading. Many currency funds have institutional investors and may trade as much as $1 billion in a given currency in one day. Banks that operate in Eurocurrency markets should be aware of the potential losses that can arise from a practice by fund managers that is known as being "lined up." For example, a fund manager may instruct its traders to sell $300 million in a currency. The order is divided into six separate orders for $50 million each. The first dealer receives a sell order for $50 million, and, in rapid succession, five other dealers are contacted. By the time the first dealer tries to sell his $50 million in the currency, the market may have moved significantly, creating an automatic loss on the trade.

Banks that act as currency dealers can protect themselves from this practice by asking the trader to reveal the size of their transactions before quoting an exchange rate. If the trader declines to reveal the size, the bank has the alternative of adjusting the rate to compensate for a potentially automatic loss as the result of being lined up.

Bond Markets

As robust as the Eurocurrency market is, growth has been even stronger in the longer-term market for Eurobonds. International bonds are either Eurobonds or foreign bonds. The major currency in the international bond market is the U.S. dollar, with rapidly growing participation in other currencies. Eurobonds developed after the Eurocurrency markets. Eurobonds are bonds that are issued by parties outside their domestic capital markets, underwritten by an international investment banking syndicate, placed in at least two countries, and, perhaps, issued in more than one currency. The firms that underwrite Eurobonds generally maintain offices in New York, London, Tokyo, and other Euromarket centers. An international underwriting syndicate and multinational placement distinguish Eurobonds from other international issues. Eurobond issuer and investor need not *necessarily* be in different countries. For example, a U.S. firm may issue a Eurobond and sell part of it to a U.S. insurance company.

In the case of foreign bonds, though, the country of origin of foreign bond issuers is *not* the same as that of the investor. Foreign bonds are issued by entities outside their own domestic capital markets in a foreign market, underwritten by a firm that is domestic to that foreign market, usually denominated in the currency of the market in which they are issued, but occasionally denominated in another currency. Foreign bonds are sometimes referred to as *traditional* international bonds because they existed long before Eurobonds. *Yankee bonds* are foreign bonds issued in the United States. Foreign bonds issued in the United Kingdom are called *Bulldog bonds*, while those issued in Japan are known as *Samurai bonds*. The Spanish variety of foreign bonds is known as *Matador bonds*, the Portuguese *Navigator bonds*, and those in Asia outside Japan *Dragon bonds*.

Immediately after World War II, the United States was the primary market for foreign bonds, but the interest rate disincentive of the Interest Equalization Tax caused much of the dollar-denominated borrowing to move to the Eurobond market. More recent trends in international bond issuance continue to favor Euromarkets.

Eurobonds denominated in dollars continue to represent the majority of issuances, even though the share has slipped somewhat. A gradual decline in the relative importance of the dollar is linked to several factors. Liberalization of regulations in the United Kingdom, Japan, Germany, and France have made international bond issuance easier. and the popularity of currency swaps has made it possible to issue Eurobonds in one currency and swap the proceeds for another currency.

Japanese issuers are increasingly prominent in the international bond market. This may be partially explained by Japan's large international trade surpluses, much of which is tied to trade with the United States. The magnitude of this dollar-denominated trade gives Japan easy access to long-term and short-term international financial markets.

A new form of the Euroband has emerged recently as the *global bond*. To qualify as a global bond, an issue must be offered in the three main geographical centers--London, New York, and Tokyo--with no restrictions. The first global bond issue was in 1989 for the World Bank. Recently, the instrument gained more acceptance as a way of raising funds for highly rated sovereign borrowers. The first such application was a $2 billion 5-year issue for the Republic of Ireland in November 1992. The market apparently viewed the issue favorably, pricing it only 52 basis points over Treasuries. The second sovereign global bond issue was that of the Kingdom of Sweden, a $2 billion 10-year flotation in February 1993. The

Province of Ontario also participated with a $2 billion issue in May 1992 led by J.P. Morgan and Salomon Brothers International.

The global bond market accelerated in 1992 (rather than 1989--after the first World Bank entry) primarily because sovereign borrowers needed to raise large amounts of capital. Global bonds appear to have an enhanced liquidity because there are more investors which, in turn, create greater demand. For example, in April 1993, two global issues of the World Bank and the Kingdom of Ireland were the most actively traded. Part of this larger market, of course, is in the United States. U.S. regulations with respect to Eurobonds have an impact on the way global bond syndicates are typically structured. U.S. investors are allowed to purchase Eurobonds only after a 40-day waiting period, unless the borrower qualifies for an exemption. The waiting period is waived if:

- The borrower does not have a substantial market interest in the United States, that is, its debt is not held by more than 300 U.S. persons, *and*
- More than $1 billion and 20% of the outstanding debt of the borrower is not held in the United States.

U.S. investors that reside outside the United States are not subject to the rule. Thus, as many as 25 U.S. investment funds have overseas offices through which they buy Eurobonds. Nevertheless, the participation by U.S. investors is greatly enhanced when the bond is also issued in the United States, as is the case with a global bond.

To facilitate issuance in the United States, a U.S. institution is almost always retained to assist in the Securities and Exchange Commission (SEC) registration. Not infrequently, the issue is denominated in U.S. dollars and this has become a point of contention. On one hand, U.S. institutions take the position that the global bond is a way to create a kind of international currency. On the other hand, Europeans banks consider the global bond to be a ploy on the part of U.S. institutions to break into European markets. The continued debate should prove interesting particularly since the World Bank and Crédit Local de France plan to issue global issues denominated in deutsche marks and French francs, respectively.

It is commonly believed that a global bond issue is appropriate for at least a $1 billion issue with perhaps an upper bound of $5 billion. However, it is possible that the vehicle could be used for smaller issues as well. For example, the World Bank was successful with a New Zealand dollar bond in the amount of NZ$ 250 million (U.S.$ 135 million). The bond trades in the

U.S. market, the Euromarket, and the home market. As such, it is highly liquid.

The global bond promises to be an interesting component of the Euromarkets for large and small borrowers.

Commercial Paper Market

A relatively new short-term instrument in international arena is *Eurocommercial paper*, another offshoot of the Eurocurrency markets. Eurocommercial paper is short-term unsecured notes issued by firms in markets outside their domestic markets. This instrument is one of the more recent to develop in Euromarkets. Throughout the 1970s and early 1980s, both U.S. and foreign borrowers relied heavily on the U.S. commercial paper market. Even though the first issue of Eurocommercial paper was in 1970 by an American firm, this form of financing did not gain widespread acceptance until 1985.

Arrangements that permit an issuer to request immediate sale of the paper or that allow a securities dealer to solicit an issue when the timing is most advantageous have made the market more appealing as an alternative to short-term bank loans. Advances in communications technology have made precise timing of the issues possible. In addition, commercial paper interest rates compare favorably with other sources of financing.

The structure of Eurocommercial paper is not exactly the same as U.S. commercial paper. While U.S. commercial paper ranges in maturity from 25 to 270 days, Eurocommercial paper usually has an original maturity of six months. U.S. commercial paper is a simple instrument that is backed by a bank line of credit. Eurocommercial paper is a more complex financial contract with no comparable guarantee. Lastly, U.S. commercial paper is typically a physical document. But Eurocommercial paper is increasingly issued in book-entry form, that is, with electronic record-keeping only.

Euronotes are similar to Eurocommercial paper except that they include an additional agreement, a *Euronote facility* by an underwriter to place the issuer's notes, when issued, for a specified period of time. This makes a Euronote facility a medium-term credit arrangement.

Floating rate notes (FRNs) are long-term obligations with a variable interest rate. The interest rate is usually tied to LIBOR, the London Interbank Offering Rate, but most FRNs guarantee a minimum rate of return.

During the 1980s, this market expanded rapidly. After its

acceptance in 1985, Eurocommercial paper grew to an almost $60 billion industry one year later, more than double the size of Euronote issues.

Equities

Another segment of international financial markets that experienced rapid growth followed by contraction during the 1980s is the *Euroequities* market, where common and preferred stocks are offered outside the issuer's domestic capital market in one or more foreign markets and underwritten by an international syndicate. Issuing equities outside the home country market is not a new practice; firms have often floated stock issues in other countries when their domestic market was too small to absorb a large issue. In many cases, firms have issued stock in London or other major capital markets.

Euroequities are differentiated from these more traditional international issues by the nature of the underwriting syndicate. The same network of investment firms and banks that has been active in the Eurobond market is now underwriting equity issues. To the extent that an issue or a portion of an issue is offered through such an international syndicate, it is a Euroequity issue. As is true with other Euromarkets, the home of the Euroequity market is London.

Frequently, large corporations issue two or more tranches, that is, groups of identical or similar securities, each offered under slightly different terms and conditions or being distributed in different ways. A multinational firm may offer domestic and international tranches, for example, with the international tranche distributed through a Euromarket syndicate, thereby qualifying as a Euroequity.

The best candidates for this form of distribution are firms that have an international product market, so that name recognition abroad will help ensure adequate investor interest. International placement helps issuing firms receive a price that is determined by worldwide market conditions and to diversify across a wider shareholder base. Firms from Germany, the United Kingdom, Italy, Switzerland, the United States, and France represent a large percentage of Euroequities issued.

Historically, the Euroequity market has been a primary market, with most secondary trading occurring in the domestic market of the issuer. The volume of secondary market trades outside the home market is increasing, however. This pattern indicates acceptance of the benefit of international diversification in managing investment portfolio risk.

The existence and operation of Euromarkets is changing the fundamental nature of banking. No longer can commercial banks consider their competition to be other domestic institutions. Increasingly, the quality of their service and the pricing of their products is being held to international standards. The internationalization of banking standards and practices has been an important influence in the deregulation of the banking industry in the United States and abroad.

Deregulation

In the wake of the high and volatile interest rates of the 1970s, commercial banks and other depository institutions found themselves at a competitive disadvantage in financial services markets. As market interest rates rose and mutual funds and securities firms began to compete with commercial banks and savings and loan associations, the flow of funds to depository institutions declined.

The Need for Change

Money market mutual funds offer small savers market rates of interest for a substantially smaller investment than once required. The funds then pool these small investments to purchase Treasury securities, large bank certificates of deposit (not subject to interest rate ceilings after 1970), commercial paper, and bankers' acceptances. Individual investors not only earned high rates of return but also received limited check writing privileges. In 1974, U.S. money market funds controlled roughly $2 billion in assets; by 1980, the total was $200 billion, and, by 1999, $1.2 trillion. The growth of these funds was one of the major motivations behind elimination of deposit interest rate regulation in the United States.

Securities firms too offered transactions accounts in direct competition with bank checking accounts. Besides earning interest on their accounts, clients received a full range of brokerage services. Competition from these two sources resulted in *disintermediation*, that is, the withdrawal of funds from depository institutions for the purpose of investing in other vehicles. Two U.S. government studies analyzed the problems of depository institutions and made specific recommendations to address them.

In 1971, the *President's Commission on Financial Structure and Regulation (the Hunt Commission)* suggested that savings and loan associations, credit unions, and mutual savings banks be permitted to offer transactions accounts. The Hunt Commission also recommended that deposit interest rate ceilings (Regulation Q) be eliminated after a phase-out period and reinstated only if necessary.

Of course, eliminating ceilings was feasible only if investment powers were also expanded. Institutions had to have the power to make investments that would earn high enough rates of return to provide a reasonable margin over deregulated deposit interest rates. In order to put all depository institutions on an equal footing, the commission suggested instituting uniform reserve requirements and giving the Federal Reserve regulatory authority over all such institutions.

In 1975, the House Banking Committee conducted the *Financial Institutions and the Nation's Economy (FINE) Study*. Several of its recommendations coincided with those of the Hunt Commission:

- Thrift institutions (savings and loan associations and mutual savings banks) should receive broader investment powers.
- Reserve requirements should be uniform.
- Deposit interest rate ceilings should be eliminated.

The study suggested furthermore that regulatory and insurance functions be consolidated. Even with this unanimity of opinion, federal legislation was not enacted for several years after these studies.

In 1979 inflation had been fueled by Federal Reserve monetary policy that kept interest rates low. Even so, stagnant economic growth persisted. The Federal Reserve shifted its emphasis from interest rate control toward control of monetary aggregates to discourage further expansion of the money supply. This forced depository institutions to operate in a regulatory environment that was out of step with the rest of the market. Maintaining deposit interest rate ceilings, as other market interest rates found their natural level, was inconsistent policy. Competitive pressures mounted until depository institutions were essentially in crisis.

Commercial banks withdrew from Federal Reserve membership at an unprecedented rate. Nonmember state banks had the advantages of often lower reserve requirements and the freedom to invest reserves in interest-bearing investments (unlike those held at Federal Reserve banks). The Federal Reserve became concerned that such wholesale defection would impair its ability to implement monetary policy.

The U.S. Federal Home Loan Bank Board, then the chief regulator of savings and loan associations, also pressed for reform. The deposit instruments S&Ls could offer were hardly competitive under the circumstances. Individual S&L managers also sought expanded deposit and investment powers.

Even consumer groups lobbied for deregulation. They argued that Regulation Q discriminated against small investors. Since 1970, the deposit rate ceilings for certificates of deposit in excess of $100,000 had been eliminated. Only rates paid to small depositors were still maintained at artificially low levels.

At the state level, mutual savings banks had won the right to offer NOW (negotiable order of withdrawal) accounts that were in fact interest-bearing checking accounts. However, such permission had been won primarily in the Northeast, the region in which mutual savings banks are concentrated; NOW accounts were not available nationwide. The U.S. Congress had little alternative. In 1980, the first major legislative overhaul of depository institutions since the 1930s was carried out.

Legislative Changes

The *Depository Institutions Deregulation and Monetary Control Act of 1980*, DIDMCA, provided for expanded asset and liability powers and, simultaneously, increased the authority of the Federal Reserve.[10] Its main features are listed below.

- New reserve requirements for both member and nonmember commercial banks were set. This provision virtually eliminates the motivation to withdraw from the Federal Reserve.
- The Federal Reserve was instructed to provide services to all depository institutions, including access to the discount window.
- The reserve requirements applicable to commercial banks were applied to other depository institutions. Savings and loans associations, mutual savings banks, and credit unions are now subject to uniform reserve requirements.
- The Federal Reserve was instructed to establish a schedule of fees for services. Prior to DIDMCA, there were generally no fees.

---

[10] The DIDMCA is also known as the Monetary Control Act of 1980 and as the Omnibus Banking Act.

- The Depository Institutions Deregulation Committee (DIDC) was created to oversee the phase-out of Regulation Q deposit interest rate ceilings over a six-year period. Voting members of the DIDC were Secretary of the Treasury, and the chairs of the Federal Reserve, the Federal Deposit Insurance Corporation, the Federal Home Loan Bank Board, and the National Credit Union Administration. The Comptroller of the Currency was a nonvoting member.
- Interest-bearing transactions accounts became legal products for all depository institutions. All banks and thrifts could offer negotiable order of withdrawal (NOW) accounts. Credit unions were permitted to offer share drafts. Only individuals and nonprofit organizations, however, could take advantage of NOW accounts and the interest rate was set at slightly over 5%.
- The limit of insurance for accounts in depository institutions was raised from $40,000 to $100,000.
- S&Ls could now offer credit cards and were permitted to make commercial real estate loans and consumer loans, each up to 20% of total assets.
- Mutual savings banks could make business loans and offer demand accounts to business clients.
- State usury laws were effectively eliminated for mortgage, business, and agricultural loans.

With the DIDMCA, the scope of Federal Reserve authority has been expanded from state bank members to *all* U.S. depository institutions. Depository institutions are more competitive in that they may now offer interest-bearing checking accounts. The legislation mandated the phased-out elimination of all deposit interest rate ceilings and allowed S&Ls and mutual savings banks to move into more diversified and profitable, albeit more risky, lines of business. At the same time, the deposit insurance ceiling increased by 150%. In other words, as more potential risk was introduced into depository institutions, the government safety net expanded--a dangerous combination.

Problems in the thrift industry did not completely disappear, of course. Moreover, both commercial banks and thrifts continued to operate at a competitive disadvantage vis-à-vis money market mutual funds, whose rates of return to investors were not constrained in any way. Legislation in 1982 attempted to correct these deficiencies.

The *Garn-St Germain Depository Institutions Act of 1982* sought to expand financial institutions' powers still more and to facilitate the rescue of failing institutions. Its major provisions are:

- The money market deposit account (MMDA) was legalized for depository institutions. MMDAs could compete directly with money market mutual funds.
- Federal, state, and local governments were permitted to own NOW accounts.
- Federally chartered S&Ls were empowered to offer demand accounts to persons or organizations with whom they had business relationships.
- The DIDC was instructed to eliminate (Regulation A) deposit rate differentials between commercial banks and thrifts.
- Savings and loan associations were permitted to diversify asset portfolios further, up to certain percentages of total assets: a.commercial real estate loans, 40%: secured and unsecured commercial loans, 5%; commercial leasing 10%; consumer loans, 30%.
- Savings and loan associations could add state and local government revenue bonds to their asset portfolios. Before 1982, only investments in general obligation bonds were allowed.
- Federal regulators received more financial and geographic flexibility for rescuing thrifts, making it possible for financial and nonfinancial firms to purchase thrifts on more favorable terms for the buyers.
- The percentage of capital that a national bank could lend to a single borrower was increased from 10% to 15%, plus an additional 10% for loans collateralized by readily marketable assets.
- National banks were permitted to form bank service companies and to invest in export trading firms. These provisions gave national banks more operational flexibility.
- The transfer of assets (excluding low-quality assets) between bank holding companies and affiliated banks was substantially liberalized.
- The Federal Deposit Insurance Corporation (FDIC), the Federal Savings and Loan Insurance Corporation (FSLIC), and the National Credit Union Administration (NCUA) were instructed to study the Federal deposit insurance system and to identify and evaluate possible alternatives.

The Garn St Germain Act made it easier for regulators to close failing thrift institutions. Under the Act, depository institutions can now compete directly with money market funds, by offering a similar instrument *with* deposit insurance coverage. For commercial banks, lending limits to individual customers were increased and the scope of activities expanded. S&Ls powers were so transformed that, at least in terms of statutory powers, it became difficult to distinguish S&Ls from commercial banks.

Even these expanded powers did not bring an end to the problems in the savings and loan and commercial banking industries. In fact, the 1980s would witness bank and S&L failure rates that had not seen since the 1930s.

The Deposit Insurance Crisis

In 1989, the U.S. Congress was compelled to restructure the deposit insurance system and make major changes in regulatory oversight. The federal deposit insurance agencies that were created in the early 1930s have only recently been seriously challenged. During the 37 years from 1943 through 1979, only 210 banks failed. But in the six-year period ended 1985, 300 failed. Another 769 failed between 1986 and 1989. Thus, in the 1980s, over 1,000 banks failed, five times the number of failures in the previous four decades. Contraction of the savings and loan industry has been even more severe. S&Ls numbered over 5,000 in 1979. By 1989, only 3,000 remained and currently the number is closer to 1,700.

Not all the bank failures were handled in the same way. When the troubled bank is large, it is more likely that all depositors and creditors will be paid by the FDIC. The controversial arrangement for large banks is attributed to the "too big to fail" theory of deposit insurance. In essence, it means that depositors in large institutions have implicit insurance on all deposits, including those with balances in excess of $100,000, and that general creditors (without the status of deposits) will also face no loss. The concept is controversial because it:

- involves differential treatment of bank depositors by a government agency
- discourages depositors in large banks from forcing market discipline on those banks, as the depositors are remain confident that their investments are safe regardless of bank behavior
- causes depositors to have less confidence in small banks, thereby making them less competitive

- greatly increases the exposure of FDIC to loss, thereby indirectly exposing the U.S. taxpayers to greater loss

The FDIC's reason for handling large troubled banks in this way is the potential effect to the banking system as a whole should a large bank fail. A large bank failure could bring systemwide instability and bank runs. The cost of this instability is thought to be greater than the cost of an unconditional bank bailout.

The first instance of this special treatment was Continental Illinois National Bank in 1984, with liabilities of $33 billion, of which only $3 billion were insured. All claims of depositors and creditors were completely guaranteed by the government. To rescue the bank, the coordinated efforts of the FDIC, the Federal Reserve, and a private bank syndicate were necessary.

The Bank of New England was allowed to fail, but FDIC was there with the same spirit of assistance as in the case of Continental. In the two years before it collapsed in January 1991, the Bank of New England lost $600 million. The bank was pulled down by the region's downward economic spiral, bankrupt companies, and vacant real estate. The prospects for the Bank of New England were so dismal that only three bidders participated in the auction--Fleet Financial Group, Bank of America, and Bank of Boston. Fleet won with a $625 million bid.

The FDIC agreed to absorb any losses attributable to Bank of New England's troubled loans, set up a special "bad bank" to hold these loans, and paid Fleet to liquidate them. The FDIC may not step in every case to this extent, but it is clear that certain larger banks will always warrant special treatment to minimize the market disruption that may be associated with their failure.

In the savings and loan industry, there are no institutions that are too big too fail. In fact, most have historically operated with relatively little regulatory oversight. The new powers of the 1980 and 1982 legislation combined with higher deposit insurance, were tailor-made for abuse in a lax regulatory climate. Many S&Ls attracted *brokered deposits*, large certificates of deposit (CDs) sold through securities brokers. Since the CDs were completely insured as long as the deposit did not exceed $100,000, investors were confident that their money was safe and asked few questions about the soundness of the S&L. The S&L had a ready source of cash then to invest in new activities permitted to it, including junk bonds, commercial loans, commercial real estate loans, and direct real estate investments. The originally conservative residential mortgage finance industry was transformed into a free-wheeling, high risk money machine, completely insured by the federal government.

The failure rate became so high that the *Financial Institutions Reform, Recovery, and Enforcement Act (FIRREA)* was passed in August 1989. Under the strain of widespread failures, the Federal Savings and Loan Insurance Corporation (FSLIC) was declared insolvent and absorbed by the FDIC. The fund that insures savings and loan associations is still maintained separately from the bank insurance fund. Under the FDIC, the S&L fund is designated the Savings Association Insurance Fund (SAIF).

But FDIC resources had also been strained. Bank failures had accelerated because of Third World bank loans and domestic loans in the oil and gas and commercial real estate sectors. The Bank Insurance Fund (BIF--the renamed FDIC fund), which stood at $18 billion at the beginning of 1988, fell to $11.4 as of June 1990.

The FDIC Assessment Rate Act of 1990 gave the FDIC board broad authority to set premiums in order to maintain desired reserves to deposit ratios for the BIF and SAIF. By 1991, the fund balance was down to $8.4 billion and in danger of being depleted if not for injection of new capital. The FDIC Improvement Act of 1991 gave the FDIC the power to borrow $70 billion from the Treasury Department and from member banks.

In 1989 FIRREA had mandated that the FDIC adjust insurance premiums so that the fund balance be maintained at an amount between 1.25% and 1.40% of estimated insured deposits. At the end of 1989, the ratio of insurance fund balance to insured deposits was only 0.70%. By June 1990, the ratio stood even lower at 0.57%.

To reverse this trend, deposit insurance premiums have gone from 0.083% of deposits before FIRREA to 0.195% of deposits in 1991 and, according to provisions in FIRREA, could go as high as 0.325%. The FDIC Improvement Act also stipulated that the weighted average bank assessment may not fall below .23 percent for deposits until the ratio of fund balance to insured deposits reached 1.25 percent.

At the same time that FSLIC was absorbed by FDIC, the Federal Home Loan Bank Board, once essentially an independent agency, was converted into the Office of Thrift Supervision (OTS) and brought under the authority of the Treasury Department.

Those S&Ls that had been closed by federal regulators and others, in unstable financial condition but still open because FSLIC lacked the funds to close them, became the responsibility of the Resolution Trust Corporation (RTC), created by FIRREA to liquidate failed savings institutions. FIRREA mandated that the RTC would operate only until December 31, 1996.

FIRREA attempted to correct some of the excesses of the early 1980s legislation by requiring higher capital levels and more prudent investment policies for thrifts, shoring up the federal insurance fund, and limiting the use of brokered deposits.

FDIC Improvement Act of 1991

The FDIC Improvement Act (FDICIA) of 1991 mandated that risk-based insurance assessments be developed by FDIC no later than January 1994. According to this legislation, BIF assessments were not permitted to fall below 0.23% of deposits until the ratio of fund balance to insured deposits reached 1.25%. FDICIA required that such restoration of the BIF be achieved within 15 years of enactment of the legislation. For the SAIF, the 1.25% ratio was to be achieved within 20 years of enactment.

Also, FDICIA permitted the FDIC to borrow up to $70 billion from the U.S. Treasury Department and from member banks to fund resolution of troubled institutions. However, the average BIF and SAIF assessment rates were not permitted to fall below 0.23% and 0.15%, respectively, until the 1.25% fund balance-to-insured deposits had been achieved and any borrowings repaid.

Restoration of the U.S. Insurance Funds

In May 1995, the BIF had repaid its borrowings (approximately $30 billion) and had achieved the 1.25% fund balance-to-insured deposits ratio. The SAIF achieved this status as of September 30, 1996. By mid-1998, the BIF and the SAIF amounted to $28.9 billion and $9.6 billion, respectively. In 1998, insurance assessments for both funds were based on capital ratios and on overall ratings of risk. With the funds officially recapitalized, assessment rates were set between 0% and 0.27%. The deposit insurance funds have been restored to health and the wave of failures in the industry has ended.

Deregulation in Other Countries

While Swiss and German universal banks have long been permitted a full range of activities, the United Kingdom, Canada, and Japan have made significant strides in liberalizing their financial markets. This trend toward deregulation will affect banking business for the foreseeable future.

In the *United Kingdom*, the 1971 Competition and Credit Regulations of the Bank of England dismantled the interest rate cartel of clearing banks, with the primary objective of placing financial institutions on more equal footing. In a sense, these regulations were precursors of the 1980 U.S. Monetary Control Act. The Bank of England regulations have resulted in more vigorous competition among clearing banks and, in general, among all financial institutions. Banks are now permitted to operate as primary dealers in the market for Treasury securities.

The "Big Bang" of 1986 fundamentally changed the U.K. financial system in that banks were given the right to invest in securities firms. Mergers within the commercial and investment banking circles of London have created clearing banks that are becoming "universal" banks that offer a full range of financial services. Building societies (savings and loan associations) may sell mutual fund shares, offer credit cards, and compete in banking services. The shares of new and small companies may now trade on the London Stock Exchanges Third Market, created in 1987. In 1999, financial services regulation in the United Kingdom was brought under one umbrella structure that united banking, securities and insurance oversight to mirror the formation of firms with all aspects of financial activities.

Competition among *Canadian* financial institutions has increased since 1967, as a result of the Canadian Bank Act. The act removed deposit rate ceilings and granted expanded lending powers to depository institutions. Chartered (commercial) banks began to offer deposits at market rates of interest and to cultivate mortgage and consumer loan business.

Foreign bank entry into the Canadian market had been difficult because of the high concentration of assets in the five largest banks and because of the close relationship of these five with the government. However, the 1980 Bank Act introduced a new type of bank, a Schedule B bank. Banks already existing were designated Schedule A banks. New Canadian-owned banks may be incorporated as Schedule A or Schedule B banks. No more than 10% of the shares of a Schedule A bank may be held by one party. On the other hand, as long as the capital of a Schedule B bank does not exceed $750 million, the 10% ownership restriction does not apply. This means that foreign banks may now enter the Canadian market under this Schedule B framework and establish a subsidiary that may remain closely held as long as capital does not exceed $750 million.

The heavily regulated system of *Japan* has been liberalized, but not to the same extent. Previously denied access to money markets, commercial banks have enjoyed expanded powers since the late 1970s, notably the right to issue negotiable certificates of deposit (NCD). Banking reform in 1982 was the most comprehensive in over 50 years. Since 1982, Japanese banks have been permitted to purchase, sell, and underwrite government securities. Subsequent regulatory changes have allowed even more flexibility in banks' money market operations. The Euro-yen NCD was authorized in 1984 and the yen bankers' acceptance market permitted a year later. In 1985, banks were permitted to offer money market certificates with interest tied to money market rates. In the same year, interest rate ceilings were liberalized for deposits of ¥1 billion or more and then liberalized for deposits of ¥500 million in 1986.

Deregulation is a common theme in many financial markets today. As noted earlier, the increased interaction among markets makes these changes necessary to maintain and enhance competitive position. Deregulation in individual countries, however, ultimately will not have the same impact as the more sweeping implications of the Single European Market.

The European Union

Barriers to free capital movement across national borders are being torn down. Perhaps the most significant instance of dissolution of capital barriers is the creation of a Single European Market among the countries of the European Union.

The European Economic Community (EEC) Treaty of 1957, also called the Treaty of Rome, united Belgium, France, Italy, Luxembourg, the Netherlands, and Germany for the purpose of coordinating monetary policies and actions for their mutual benefit. In 1965, the EEC joined with two other European industrial associations (the European Coal and Steel Community and the European Atomic Energy Community) and became the European Community (EC).[11]

---

[11] The European Coal and Steel Community was created by the Treaty of Paris in 1951 with the goal of transferring control of the materials of war from national governments to multilateral institutions. The founding countries were the six that signed the Treaty of Rome.

In 1973, Denmark, the Irish Republic, and the United Kingdom joined the EC. Greece became a member in 1981, Portugal and Spain in 1986. Austria, Finland, and Sweden joined in 1995. The total number of EC members is 15 and the total population of these 15 countries is 369 million. The designation for the member countries is now the European Union (EU), signifying even closer coordination of their political and monetary policies.

Development of the Single European Market

Before 1985, the integration of Europe was to be effected through the harmonization of national rules and regulations. This meant that each EC member was to adopt identical rules and regulations--a difficult process at best. To overcome the difficulty, the Commission issued proposals in 1985 in a document entitled *Completing the Internal Market: White Paper from the Commission to the European Council.* The 1985 White Paper recommended that the concept of harmonization be replaced, in many cases, with the concept of mutual recognition. Under mutual recognition, it is not necessary for each member country to adopt exactly the same rules and regulations. Instead, each member country is required to recognize the validity of the rules and regulations of other member countries. Of course, over time, the assumption was that mutual recognition would lead to the convergence of regulatory structures, that is, harmonization. The 1985 White Paper contained a list of 300 (later reduced to 279) specific measures for implementing general principles. In 1986, the Single European Act was passed to implement the White Paper recommendations. This act created the Single European Market, effective January 1, 1992.

In February 1992, the EC Ministers met in Maastricht (the Netherlands) and signed a treaty (the Maastricht Treaty) that:

- Expanded the powers to the European Parliament (567 members elected by the EU countries).
- Allowed the European Community to form common foreign and defense policies for the first time.
- Formed the European Union.

The formation of the EU through treaties and directives (that are binding on the EU members) has had a profound effect on the banking industry and the operation of financial markets.

Banking Directives and the Single Passport

The First Banking Directive on Coordination of Credit Institutions (1977) was the beginning of Community-wide standards for banks. In this directive, "credit institutions" are defined as any firms that receive deposits or other repayable funds from the public and that grant credits for their own accounts. The First Banking Directive confers the right to establish a credit institution, suggests various financial ratios for such firms, and encourages the supervision of institutions (that operate in several European countries) through cooperative efforts among EU members.

The Consolidated Supervision Directive of 1983 addresses the question of supervision (regulation) of credit institutions across national borders within the EU. It stipulates that when one institution owns more than 25% of another, the two institutions shall be supervised on a consolidated basis. The supervisor of such institutions must review the accounts, exposure, and management of the consolidated institution at least on a yearly basis.

The Second Banking Directive on Coordination of Credit Institutions created the *single banking license*, or *single passport*. This directive, adopted in 1989 and effective January 1, 1993, builds on the First Banking Directive and the Consolidated Supervision Directive.

With a license issued in any one of the EU countries, a bank may operate throughout the EU. The activities in which a bank may engage include commercial banking, leasing, securities trading, securities underwriting, and financial advising. If the home country of a credit institution permits these activities, the institution may provide these services throughout the EU.

Two limits are stipulated in connection with credit institutions acquiring nonfinancial businesses:

- A credit institution may not hold a stake in a nonfinancial business that exceeds 10 percent of its capital.
- The total value of all such stakes may not exceed 50% of the institution's capital.

In order for a credit institution from outside the EU to obtain a single passport into the EU, that firm must own or establish a subsidiary in one of the EU countries. Foreign institutions with subsidiaries that were established before the Second Banking Directive are grandfathered (permitted to continue operations) and may enjoy the full benefits of the single passport. It is also possible for a bank from a non-EU country to maintain only a branch in one of the EU members. However, such a branch will not enjoy the privileges of the single passport.

The Second Banking Directive also establishes the minimum capital required to establish a credit institution. A parent institution must have a capital base of at least Ecu5 million (about $6.2 million).[12] However, once a parent has been established in one of the EU countries, it may branch into the other EU countries with no additional capital investment required.

The Own Funds Directive defines capital for credit institutions. The Solvency Ratios Directive incorporates the definition of capital into a minimum ratio that all credit institutions must attain. In conformity with international capital standards, the minimum ratio of capital to assets is 8%. Both these directives became effective on January 1, 1993.

Economic and Monetary Union

The Second Banking Directive (and those directives related to it) moves the European Union toward harmonization of rules governing credit institutions and toward cross-border operation with minimal obstructions. In addition, the EU has taken a major step toward economic and monetary union (EMU) with the introduction of a single currency for 11 of the 15 EU members.

The European Monetary System

In 1979, the *European Monetary System (EMS)* was established through a resolution of the European Council. The objective was to create a zone of increasing monetary stability within Europe.

The *European Currency Unit (Ecu)* was created. The Ecu was a GNP-weighted basket of member currencies, whose composition changed as the result of adjustments every five years.

Some of the EC members agreed to intervene in the foreign exchange market to correct greater than agreed upon swings in individual currency values as compared to the Ecu. This new arrangement was called the *Exchange Rate Mechanism (ERM)*. Not all EU Members were members of the ERM, even though they were members of the EMS.

The European Monetary Cooperation Fund was established to issue Ecus against member country deposits of gold and foreign exchange.

---

[12] The ECU is the European Currency Unit, a basket of EU currencies. See the following section.

The Ecu served several functions--including the unit of account for the system and the basis for the divergence indicator. The Ecu was first used to denominate and settle central bank debts and claims of member countries. By 1989, the Ecu had become one of the top five currencies most frequently used in international transactions. Also in 1989, Luxembourg became the first EU country to encourage use of the Ecu in everyday transactions. In 1998, it was possible for private citizens to buy travellers' checks in Ecus, maintain bank accounts in Ecus, purchase Ecu-based mutual fund shares, obtain Ecu loans and mortgages, and have credit card purchases denominated in Ecus.

The maximum variation of a member country currency rate was set at plus or minus 2.25% of its value in terms of Ecus--the *parity limit*, with the *divergence indicator* set at 75% of this maximum spread. When the divergence indicator was reached, the member country was obliged to intervene in currency markets and, generally, take steps to bring its currency within the agreed upon range of values.

Parity limits defined the maximum amount by which a currency could move within the ERM. They were derived from *cross-parity rates.* Dividing one central Ecu rate by another yielded the target cross-parity rate between each pair of currencies. Divergence indicators were defined in terms of the value of a currency relative to the Ecu and were intended to reflect the overall strength within the ERM. Divergence indicators were 75% of the deviation that would put a currency at its limits against every currency in the Ecu.

In 1988, an EC Committee was asked to study the process of creating a unified European currency. The resulting *Delors Committee Report,* accepted in 1989, recommended that conversion to a totally unified currency take place in three stages:

Stage 1:

A period of closer coordination and full participation of EC members in the Exchange Rate Mechanism.

Stage 2:

A transition phase during which (a) the central banks (monetary authorities) of EC countries would more closely coordinate monetary policy and (b) the framework for a European central bank, a kind of "Eurofed", would be established.

Stage 3:
The final point when the "Eurofed" assumes full control of European monetary policy and a single European currency circulates in lieu of existing national currencies.

The objectives of monetary union were frustrated when the United Kingdom and Denmark withdrew from the ERM in the fall of 1992, delaying completion of Stage 2. For reasons related to the German reunification in 1990, Germany had maintained high interest rates to both attract capital and to control inflation. This caused the value of the deutsche mark to remain high vis-à-vis other EC currencies. The cost of maintaining agreed upon parities--in terms of both market intervention and maintenance of high interest rates--was too high and the United Kingdom and Denmark pulled out. For a period of time, currency exchange markets were in turmoil and serious doubts arose as to the feasibility of a true monetary union in Europe.

Since that time, German interest rates have fallen, easing some of the pressure on other European countries to maintain high interests to the detriment of their national economies. Also, the Exchange Rate Mechanism was "temporarily" modified in August 1993 such that most member countries were required just to maintain their currencies within 15% of parity (above or below). Only Germany and the Netherlands remain subject to the original fluctuation bands. This modification effectively returned the member currencies to floating rate status, but it also kept the ERM at least nominally intact.

The Maastricht Treaty

Effective November 1993, the Maastricht Treaty outlined an important framework for transition from *monetary system* to *monetary union*. The treaty stipulated January 1, 1994 as the date for commencement of Stage 2 of monetary union. During Stage 2, the *European Monetary Institute (EMI)* replaced the Committee of Central Bank Governors (which had presided over monetary coordination). The EMI was located in Frankfurt, Germany and, among other things:

Took over the administration of the European Monetary Cooperation Fund (which issued Ecus) and the accompanying financing mechanisms.

- Monitored the operation of the EMS.
- Facilitated use of private Ecu.
- Oversaw development of the Ecu clearing system.

- Was consulted by national authorities on monetary policy and helped draft legislation on the eventual convergence of all currencies into one currency.

All EU central banks were members of the EMI. The organization was intended to strengthen the coordination of the member states' monetary policies in preparation for Stage 3 of monetary union. Also during Stage 2, a *European System of Central Banks (ESCB)* was formed, with the *European Central Bank (ECB)* as a the principal new monetary institution. At the beginning of Stage 3, the EMI was liquidated and the European Central Bank assumed it functions. The formation of the new system follows guidelines established by the Committee of Central Bank Governors (predecessor of the European Monetary Institute).

The European System of Central Banks and the European Central Bank assumed their full powers under Stage 3 and are responsible for issuing and managing the single currency that eventually will replace the national currencies. The United Kingdom, Denmark, and Sweden elected not to converge on January 1, 1999, that is, did not automatically join Stage 3. Greece will join upon meeting the full criteria for convergence.[13] In order to join Stage 3, a member state must:

- Achieve a high degree of price stability. The average one-year inflation rate before examination by EU authorities must not exceed by more than 1.5 percentage points the inflation rate of the three best performing EU members.
- Demonstrate sustainability of its government financial position. An excessive government deficit can disqualify an EU country from convergence. Public deficits may not exceed 3% of GDP, while total public debt may not exceed 60% of GDP.
- Observe the normal fluctuation margins provided by the Exchange Rate Mechanism for at least two years without devaluing its currency against the currency of another EU member.
- Demonstrate adequate control of its interest rates. For one year prior to examination by EU authorities, the long-term government bond (or comparable) interest rate may not exceed by more than 2 percentage points the long-term government bond rate of the three best performing EU members.

---

[13] The eleven converging countries on January 1, 1999 were Austria, Belgium, Finland, France, Germany, Ireland, Italy, Luxembourg, the Netherlands, Portugal, and Spain.

These criteria have been established for joining Stage 3 of monetary union, but one could argue that the criteria are desirable goals in a national policy making context. Domestic price stability, adequate control of government finance, proper management of the external value of domestic currency, and a reasonable interest rate environment are conditions in any event for which every sovereign state strives.

In December 1995, the EU heads of government met in Madrid, reaffirming January 1, 1999 as commencement of European Monetary Union. The leaders decided that the name of the new currency would be the *Euro*. Those countries that are members of the monetary union beginning in January 1999 were asked to issue their tradable, government debt in Euros to create a reasonably large pool of financial instruments denominated in the new currency. Nontradeable debt may continue to be denominated in the national currency during the transition period. Commercial banks have the option of accepting deposits and opening transactions accounts in the new currency prior to the mandatory change-over date of 2002.

Euro currency and coins will begin circulation on January 1, 2002. Until that time, national currencies will circulate but their exchange rates are irrevocably fixed in terms of other national currencies and in terms of the Euro.

Conclusion

The Euromarkets have grown from primarily wholesale money markets to a wide array of short-term and long-term financial services and instruments. In general, growth in Eurobonds has far outpaced the growth in traditional international bonds. Eurocommercial paper and Euronote issues expanded rapidly during the early 1980s, only to contract somewhat during the late 1980s. Primary issues in the international equity market were slowed considerably by the stock market crash of 1987, but secondary market trading has continued at a strong pace.

After the major bank legislation of the 1930s, the structure of the U.S. commercial bank system remained virtually unchanged until 1980, when depository institutions were deregulated in order to overcome competitive disadvantages vis-à-vis nondepository financial institutions. Thereafter, institutions failed at rates not seen since before the 1930s legislation. The federal agency responsible for savings and loan insurance

(FSLIC) folded. Commercial bank failures accelerated, causing assets in the commercial bank insurance fund (FDIC) to decline for the first time since its inception. The regulatory changes in oversight and deposit insurance have contributed to stabilization of the U.S. banking and thrift sectors.

Internationally, a major initiative in financial market liberalization and integration is the Single European Market. Financial firms that have been constrained by varying rules and regulations in the EC will be able to operate throughout the 15-nation region with a license from any one of them. Complete financial integration of Europe began in 1999 with the European Central Bank and the Euro.

Selected References

Abrams, Richard K., Peter K. Cornelius, Per L. Hedfors, and Gunnar Tersman. *The Impact of the European Community's Internal Market on the EFTA*, International Monetary Fund, Washington, D.C., December 1990.

Bacon, Richard. "EC Finance Rules Face Fresh Obstacles," *Euromoney*, May 1993, pp. 50-55.

Benston, George J. and George G. Kaufman. *Risk and Solvency Regulation of Depository Institutions: Past Policies and Current Options*, Salomon Brothers Center for the Study of Financial Institutions at the Graduate School of Business Administration of New York University, New York, 1988.

Binhammer, H. H. *Money, Banking, and the Canadian Financial System*, Nelson Canada, Scarborough, Ontario, 1988.

Bronte, Stephen. *Japanese Finance: Markets and Institutions*, Euromoney Publications, London, 1982.

Comparative Economic and Financial Statistics; Japan and Other Major Countries 1988, Bank of Japan, Tokyo, 1988.

Cooper, S. Kerry, and Donald R. Fraser. *Banking Deregulation and the New Competition in Financial Services*, Ballinger Publishing Company, Cambridge, Massachusetts, 1984.

"Deposit Insurance, Redux," *United States Banker*, May 1993, p. 13.

Dyer, Geogg. "Global Bonds Aim to Broaden Their Scope," *Euromoney*, June 1993, pp. 84-88.

Economic and Monetary Union, Commission of the European Communities, Luxembourg, 1990.

Einzig, Paul and Brian Scott Quinn. *The Eurodollar System; Practice and Theory of International Interest Rates*, 6th edition, St. Martin's Press, New York, 1977.

Europe 1992; The Facts, Department of Trade and Industry and the Central Office of Information, London, 1989.

European Economy; One Market, One Money; An evaluation of the potential benefits and costs of forming an economic and monetary union, Commission of the European Communities, Directorate-General for Economic and Financial Affairs, Brussels, October 1990.

Folkerts-Landau, David and Donald J. Mathieson. *The European Monetary System in the Context of the Integration of European Financial Markets*, International Monetary Fund, Washington, D.C., October 1989.

Fraser, Donald R. and Peter S. Rose, Editors. *Financial Institutions and Markets in a Changing World*, 3rd edition, Business Publications, Inc., Plano, Texas, 1987.

Grady, John, and Martin Weale. *British Banking, 1960-85*, Macmillan Press, London, 1986.

Haggar, Euan. "How the EEC Can Save the ECU Market," *Euromoney*, February 1993.

Havrilesky, Thomas M. and Robert Schweitzer, Editors. *Contemporary Developments in Financial Institutions and Markets*, Harlan Davidson, Inc., Arlington Heights, Illinois, 1987.

Huat, Tan Chwee. *Financial Institutions in Singapore*, Singapore University Press, Singapore, 1981.

International Capital Markets; Developments and Prospects, International Monetary Fund, Washington, D.C., April 1989 and April 1990.

International Monetary Fund. *International Capital Markets; Developments and Prospects*, Washington, D.C., April 1989.

"The Maastricht Agreement on Economic and Monetary Union," *Bank of England Quarterly Bulletin*, February 1992, pp. 64-68.

Modernizing the Financial System: Recommendations for Safer, More Competitive Banks, U.S. Department of the Treasury, Washington, D.C.

Mullineux, Andrew. *International Banking and Financial Systems: A Comparison*, Graham and Trotman, London, 1987.

"Recent Developments in Overseas Commercial Paper Markets," *Bank of England Quarterly Bulletin*, November 1992, p. 405.

Roman, Monica. "The New Currency Gunslingers," *Global Finance*, vol. 6, no.6 (June 1992), pp. 32-36.

Scott, Robert Haney, K.A. Wong, and Yan Ki Ho, Editors. *Hong Kong's Financial Institutions and Markets*, Oxford University Press, Hong Kong, 1986.

Smith, Geoffrey. "Fleet's Ship Comes In: Its Bank of New England Unit Has Earned Fat Profits Fast," *Business Week*, November 9, 1992, p. 104.

Subcommittee on Financial Institutions Supervision, Regulation, and Insurance. *Report of the Task Force on International Competitiveness of U.S. Financial Institutions*, U.S. House of Representatives Committee on Banking, Finance and Urban Affairs, Washington, D.C., 1990.

Tew, Brian. *The Evolution of the International Monetary System, 1945-81*, Hutchinson & Co., Ltd., London, 1982.

Ungerer, Horst, Juko J. Hauvonen, Augusto Lopez-Claros, and Thomas Mayer. *The European Monetary System: Developments and Prospectives*, International Monetary Fund, Washington, D.C., November 1990.

U.S. Securities and Exchange Commission. *Internationalization of Securities Markets; Report to the Senate Committee on Banking, Housing and Urban Affairs and the House Committee on Energy and Commerce*, Washington, D.C., 1987.

4. Regulatory Influences

Introduction

Commercial banks in the United States are among the most strictly regulated institutions. Bank regulation appears reasonable since banks are such an important part of the payments system and provide basic financial services to consumers and businesses alike. To some extent, this is also true in other countries. However, in comparison to that in other countries, the relationship between U.S. banks and regulators has been at best. In addition, in the United States, foreign banks were first ignored, then given preferential treatment, and lastly have been allowed to continue their protected activities under certain "grandfather" clauses in federal legislation.

The Need for Regulation

It cannot be denied that bank regulation is necessary to maintain the safety and soundness of banking systems in all industrialized countries. As interest rates on deposits are being deregulated, many of the remaining regulations focus on the areas of liquidity standards, loan concentrations, and capital standards.

Liquidity Standards

The adequacy of bank liquidity is tied to solvency of the banking system. From a regulatory perspective, liquidity means a bank's ability to meet its obligations when they are due. Before the widespread use of liability management, liquidity was more easily measurable. Maintaining high-quality, liquid assets gave reassurance to both the public and the regulators.

The ability to convert these assets into cash meant that even heavy deposit withdrawal could be met. In turn, this situation lead to confidence in the bank's solvency, so that "runs" were unlikely. However, it is not always possible to assess exactly the liquidity of certain assets. Municipal bonds are a good example. Large sales of municipals can depress their market value since secondary markets for municipals are not as well developed as markets for Treasury securities. Nevertheless, municipal bond yields frequently compare favorably with government bond yields (on an after-tax basis). From the bank's perspective, then, the less liquid municipal bonds may be preferable.

Another shortcoming of attempting to measure liquidity based on asset holdings is that this approach does not consider the dynamic aspect of banking. The use of active liability management began in 1961 when U.S. banks began to issue negotiable certificates of deposit as a means to more actively control funding sources. However, in 1966, regulated domestic deposit rates were not competitive with Treasury security rates. To circumvent the problem of low, noncompetitive rates, U.S. banks issued dollar-denominated negotiable CDs overseas. Since the rate ceilings did not apply to overseas deposits, competitive rates could be offered. Foreign branches raised funds that could not be raised domestically. These events gave birth to a much more active liability management and to the Eurodollar market.[14] In the case of the 1966 credit crunch measuring liquid assets as a percentage of deposits would probably not have revealed the impending problem. That is, the balance sheet alone does not reflect the ease or difficulty that a bank may have in refinancing maturing deposits or other liabilities.

Because of these considerations, many regulators have moved more to a *cash flow* approach in assessing bank liquidity. In general, cash flow techniques attempt to measure any mismatch in the maturity structure of asset and liability portfolios.

Some countries have formal requirements. Instead, liquidity review is a part of the regular oversight process. In Canada, this is accomplished through informal monitoring of maturity mismatching. In the United Kingdom, cash flow over the next 12 months is routinely reviewed.

---

[14] See also Chapter 3 for a discussion of Euromarkets.

The approach in the United States is a combination of fixed-ratio maintenance and cash flow analysis. Smaller banks are evaluated primarily on the basis of liquid asset levels. Larger banks, considered to have greater access to money and capital markets, are assessed on the basis of projected cash flow or maturity mismatches.

The CAMEL rating system is used in the United States. The specific qualities considered are:

C	Capital adequacy
A	Asset quality
M	Management and administrative ability
E	Earnings level and quality
L	Liquidity level

Each bank is scored between 1 (best) and 5 (worst). Banks with poor results are examined more frequently by federal regulators.

Loan Concentration

Regulators in the United States also examine bank loan portfolios to spot excessive concentration of *long-term loans*. While commercial banks are not precluded from making loans for 15 to 30 years, if a substantial share of the portfolio is devoted to long-term loans, the bank may be effectively taking equity positions with client firms. Such positions are, of course, to be avoided since banks *are prohibited* from holding nonfinancial corporate stock. This is particularly true if the client is not well capitalized.

The basic premise is that an excessive amount of long-term loans that have a *fixed rate of interest* can also expose the bank to risk if interest rates increase. Deposits are short-term liabilities that can quickly reflect a higher level of interest rates. If the bank holds large quantities of long-term fixed rate loans, interest expense on deposits can increase much faster than interest income on loans and put considerable strain on bank profitability.

While there is no established maximum percentage of long-term, fixed-rate loans that a bank may hold, concentration in terms of a *single borrower* is more explicitly regulated. If a bank devotes too much of its resources to one borrower, the solvency of the bank itself can depend on the financial circumstances of that client. The concept of single borrower is extended to direct and indirect obligations of the borrower. Indirect obligations include those of a partnership in which the client has ownership interest and those for which the client is an endorser or guarantor for another party. In the case of corporate clients, obligations include those of both parent and subsidiaries.

National banks in the United States may not lend more than 15% of capital to any single borrower that are not completely collateralized. If the loan is completely collateralized by readily marketable assets, the limit is 25% of capital (an additional 10%). State banks are also subject to single borrower limits, but these limits vary from one state to another.

These regulations underscore a universally recognized principle borrowed from financial theory. Diversification is an essential element for sound loan portfolio management. Significantly, in the United States, this basic goal is frustrated by the lack of a federal provision for nationwide branching.

Capital Standards

In a commercial bank, capital serves much the same functions as capital in a nonfinancial firm. It provides a *buffer for temporary operating losses.* Capital absorbs these losses until profitability is restored so that the firm remains *solvent*, that is, its assets exceed its liabilities.

Theoretically, the solvency of a bank should be determined by *market value* of assets and liabilities rather than *book value.* However, the market value of some bank assets, especially loans, is difficult to specify. Bank regulators are studying ways in which more market value accounting (MVA) can be used. As a step in the direction of full MVA, in 1991, the Financial Accounting Standards Board (FASB) framed the Statement of Financial Accounting Standards 107 (SFAS 107). This statement requires footnote disclosure of the market value of all financial instruments, including loans, for financial statements issued after December 15, 1992.[15] Other FASB pronouncements that support the trend toward market value are:

- For 1994 financial statements, SFAS 115 requires MVA (not merely footnote disclosure) for all marketable securities that are available for sale. Any associated gains or losses will be absorbed in earnings for the period. This pronouncement stops short of full MVA for marketable securities, however, because it excludes those marketable

15. The December 1992 compliance date applies to all firms with year-end assets in excess of $150 million. Smaller firms have until December 1995 to comply, although they are encouraged to comply sooner.

securities that are to be held to maturity and any related liabilities (the firm's own bonds payable).

- FAS #114 and FAS #118 are effective for statements after December 1994 and concern loan portfolio impairment. A loan is impaired when it is probable that all payments of principal and interest will not be collected. The present value of expected future cash flows is the measurement value. If the recorded value (book value) exceeds the measurement value, the excess is the amount of loan impairment and must be provided as bad debt expense for the period.
- FAS #119 required greater disclosure of derivative securities for statements issued after December 1994.
- FAS #122 required the market valuation of mortgage servicing rights after December 1995.

These are steps toward full market value accounting. Ultimately, the market value of equity will be the full basis for financial reporting. In the meantime, the book value of equity is the basis for regulatory oversight.

The ability of bank capital to absorb operating losses is not, of course, unlimited. Sustained losses will eventually erode the capital base and leave creditors' claims exposed. This will occur when cash inflows from operations (income statement activity) are insufficient to cover cash outflows. Conceptually, under these circumstances, the bank must liquidate assets in order to satisfy the shortfall (excess of expenses over revenues). As assets decline while liabilities do not, the capital base shrinks. If the process continues, asset values decline until liabilities are greater than assets. This function of capital as a cushion is common to all business organizations.

Bank capital also serves other functions that are important to regulators. Perceived capital adequacy increases *public confidence* in an institution. If public confidence is maintained, management can avoid unexpectedly high deposit withdrawals (bank runs). On the surface, bank runs may not appear to present a risk of insolvency since, presumably, the value of liquidated assets equals the value of deposits and other liabilities to be satisfied. However, when large quantities of assets must be sold quickly, the bank may realize less than asset carrying values, that is, sustain losses upon sale. These losses deplete capital in the same way as operating losses. Since a relatively small percentage of bank assets is financed with capital, liquidating as little as 5% of assets below carrying value can bring the bank close to insolvency.

Even if asset liquidation is not necessary, a loss of public confidence can increase the bank's cost of funds. If the increase is significant enough, profitability will be hurt, once again putting pressure on an already thinly capitalized institution. Thus, capital adequacy can help preserve public confidence and avoid either bank runs or high costs of doing business.

Also from a regulatory perspective, bank capital places *constraints on bank growth.* In this sense, minimum capital requirements prevent unlimited deposit taking and lending (or other investment activities). With a given capital ratio, dividend payout ratio, and rate of return on equity, a bank can expect to grow in the normal course of operating profitably.

$$\Delta TA = (ROE)(E)(b)(EM)$$

where ΔTA = change in the asset base for one year
ROE = return on equity (net income as a percentage of equity)
E = equity (dollar amount)
b = retention ratio (% of net income not paid as dividends)
EM = equity multiplier (total assets to equity)

(ROE)(E)(b) is the change in retained earnings that can be projected.[16] This addition to retained earnings forms a new equity layer that will support asset growth. When the equity multiplier is high (or the capital ratio is low), the bank's asset base can grow relatively faster. All other things being equal, regulators usually prefer to see a lower equity multiplier (higher capital ratio) because of the greater buffer against loss that it implies. Of course, regulators must seriously consider the impact of minimum capital requirements on bank profitability and competitiveness. High equity ratios also raise the cost of funds for banks and other financial institutions.

Trends in Regulation

More Formal Regulation

There are two distinctly different forms of bank regulation. The first is a *formal regulatory system*, complete with specific requirements and

---

16. (ROE)(E)(b)
= (NI/E)(E)(_retained earnings/NI)
= _retained earnings

guidelines for balance sheet ratios. The objective of such legal stipulation is to ensure stability of bank activity and monetary conditions. Examples of formal regulatory systems are those of the United States, Japan, and continental Europe.

The second type of system involves much more informal control. This is not to suggest that orderliness is a lower priority under less formal systems. Instead, the difference appears to be more related to financial system infrastructure. Where a small number of banks has existed or where banks and other financial institutions have been concentrated within a limited geographical area, a *system of non-statutory supervision* has evolved.

The geographically concentrated financial markets of the United Kingdom, Belgium, and Luxembourg are examples. Frequent interaction between senior bank management and supervisory authorities has made it possible for authorities to adequately assess bank operations and attendant risks. To the extent that such close contact has been effective, there exists little incentive to formalize the relationships.

Nevertheless, deregulation of financial services and the blurring of past lines of distinction between financial institutions has led to a trend toward *increased statutory guidelines* and even more effective oversight. The U.K. Banking Act of 1979 created a legislative framework for authorization of deposit-taking activity and supervision by the Bank of England. Before 1979, supervision was largely informal.

In Canada, there is a combination of informal and formal controls. The Canadian system developed after its U.S. counterpart, with the first commercial bank being chartered in 1817 and the Bank of Canada (central bank) not being created until 1934. This time difference allowed Canadians to observe some of the problems in the United States associated with having a large number of unit banks. Nationwide branching was accepted in Canada from the outset. As a result, five Canadian banks now control the vast majority of all bank assets. This structure makes it easy to coordinate policies with fewer laws and regulations. Formal controls consist mainly of laws that mandate public disclosure and regulate permissible bank activities. Laws have also been passed to allow supervisory authorities to issue formal regulations with respect to cash and secondary reserves, capital adequacy, and liquidity levels.

International Coordination

Another significant worldwide trend is toward greater *international cooperation* among supervisory authorities. Until the 1970s, there was no formalized international coordination. Then the Herstatt Bank, one of Germany's largest privately held banks, failed. This $900 million bank ran up foreign currency exchange losses in June 1974 that sent it to the Bundesbank for emergency funds. The Bundesbank found that the record-keeping was so poor that it could not determine the extent of loss within a short period of time. The bank was closed at 4:00 p.m., German time. New York banks were still open but unable to complete their currency transactions with the closed Herstatt. This, of course, also exposed the U.S. banks to loss. In the final accounting, Herstatt's losses amounted to $500 million. The growing interdependence of systems and the ease with which risk is sometimes spread across borders has led to more structured international communications.

The European Community (EC) has an ultimate goal of uniform bank regulation throughout the region.[17] The 1977 banking directive was the first step in this direction. Guidelines for bank licensing and supervision were to be formulated in as consistent a fashion as possible across EC members. To encourage the flow of information across borders, the second banking directive in 1989 is based on the concept of a single banking license. With one license a bank has the right to operate throughout the EC. (Similar provisions have been made for securities firms and insurance companies.) With this license, banks will be able to engage essentially in universal banking throughout the EC as long as there is "mutual recognition" in the home country of the bank.

The list of permissible activities includes:

- deposit-taking and other forms of borrowing
- financial leasing
- money transmission services
- guarantees and commitments
- trading for the bank's own account in CDs, bonds, government securities, futures and options, foreign currency and securities
- issuance of securities

---

17. This objective is part of the larger goal of creating one economic market that is composed of the twelve member nations. See Chapter 3 for a full description of the EC initiative.

- money brokering
- portfolio management
- securities safekeeping services
- credit reference services

Mutual recognition essentially means that the banks from the host country must be permitted the same scope of activities in the home country of the bank being licensed. This provision has raised serious concerns on the part of U.S. banks, given the limited scope of activity they are permitted by U.S. federal regulators vis-à-vis the scope of activity for their European counterparts.

International cooperation extends beyond the EC. The Organisation for Economic Cooperation and Development (OECD) organized the Basle Committee on Banking Regulations and Supervisory Practices to address the relevant issues of international banking. The committee's report, known as the *Basle Concordat*, was completed in 1975 and subsequently revised. It was endorsed by the regulators of the Group of Ten and Luxembourg in 1983 and subsequently endorsed by the regulators of several other countries.[18] The concordant is the basis for international coordination among banking authorities.

The two broad, primary principles of the Concordat are that (1) no foreign banking institution in a given host country should be without supervision, and (2) supervision should be adequate. The Concordat also outlines basic areas of responsibility for oversight, assigning some functions to host country authorities and others to parent country authorities.

Functional assignments are in the areas of *solvency, liquidity*, and *foreign exchange operations*. Supervision to assure solvency of foreign *branches* is the primary responsibility of the parent country. The solvency of foreign *subsidiaries* is assigned to the host country, while that of *joint ventures* falls to the country of incorporation.

The level of liquidity of both branches and subsidiaries falls within the purview of host country supervisory bodies. Again, for joint ventures, the country of incorporation is held accountable. However, the liquidity of foreign offices can affect the liquidity of the group to which it belongs. So,

---

[18] The Group of Ten consists of Belgium, Canada, France, Germany, Italy, Japan, the Netherlands, Sweden, the United States, and the United Kingdom. Switzerland is an associate member.

parent countries are held responsible for adequacy of control systems and procedures.

Lastly, foreign exchange operations are the shared responsibility of host and parent countries. The host country monitors the foreign exchange position of those institutions operating within its territory. The parent monitors the position of the entire institution.

Recently, the central bankers of major industrialized countries (the so-called Group of Seven or G7) have broached the issue of whether foreign currency markets should be more closely monitored by regulators. Volatility in currency markets has frustrated steps being taken to achieve a unified European currency. The central bankers with these concerns are led by Hans Tietmeyer, successor to Helmut Schlesinger at the Deutsche Bundesbank. The problem is that highly leveraged, unsupervised hedge funds (involved in speculative currency dealings) are trading currencies and currency futures for short-term profits and complicating the management of currency values by central banks.

Steps that have been suggested to remedy this situation include levying transactions taxes on currency trades, requiring deposits with central banks as collateral for trades, and placing a capital requirement on currency positions. Implementing any of these strategies would involve a universal and multilateral agreement. While the level of international coordination has increased substantially, there remains real doubt about the feasibility of any of these approaches. Moreover, such measures could considerably restrain the international flow of capital for all parties, not just the targeted hedge funds. As a result, it is unlikely that these measures will instituted. Instead, central banks will be forced to adapt to market conditions and fulfill their obligations for currency management through skillful trading techniques.

In general, regulators seek to coordinate their financial systems across national borders with the same objectives that operate within--safety and soundness, efficiency, and competitiveness. As these systems evolve, the changing environment will require flexibility for the oversight function to keep pace with, but not constrain, the evolution.

The Federal Reserve worked within the OECD to encourage a harmonization of capital policy among the member countries. The objectives of these coordination efforts were:

- To reduce international differences in capital levels that gave some countries competitive advantages.

- To make capital requirements sensitive to the differences in risk profiles of bank balance sheets.
- To take into account the level of off-balance sheet risk exposure.
- Remove any disincentives for holding safe, liquid assets.

As a first step, in January 1987, the Federal Reserve and the Bank of England announced an agreement on common standards of capital. Capital would be defined as:

- Equity
- Retained earnings
- Minority interest in subsidiaries
- Perpetual debt

Also, each class of assets would be weighted depending upon riskiness of the category and contingent liabilities would be included in the calculations.

The Federal Reserve and the Bank of England then attempted to get support for this scheme from other OECD members, especially France, Japan, and Germany. However, Japan and Germany resisted the plan for similar reasons. Japanese banks have significant amounts of land and equity stock recorded on their balance sheets at historical book values that are considerably below market value. Under the U.S.-U.K. plan, these "hidden" reserves could not be used to satisfy capital requirements. Likewise, German banks have large holdings of equity stock that would be considered capital. The Japanese, Germans, and French argued that defining an appropriate capital standard for all banks would be impossible.

In December of the same year, the Cooke Committee (Committee on Banking Regulation and Supervisory Practices of the Bank for International Settlements, also known as the Basel Committee) announced agreement on international convergence of capital standards. This agreement, the *Basle Accord*, addressed concerns of Japan and Germany in two ways. *Capital definitions* included asset revaluation reserves. Within prescribed limits, *risk weights* were left to the discretion of individual countries.

The definition of capital under the Basel Accord is as follows:

Tier I (core) capital:

- Shareholders' equity
- Perpetual preferred stock, net of goodwill

Tier II (supplemental) capital:

- Perpetual and term subordinated debt
- Mandatory convertible debt
- Asset revaluation reserves
- Other supplementary items at the discretion of individual countries

Tier II capital is limited to 100% of Tier I capital. According to the Accord, beginning January 1993, international banks must maintain both Tier I and Tier II capital equal to 4% of risk-weighted assets for a total capital ratio of 8%. Germany and Japan are permitted to use 45% of unrealized gains on equities held as investments toward the Tier II capital requirement. In late 1991 and early 1992, the value of Japanese equities fell dramatically because of a collapse in real estate prices and a general recession. As much as half of the unrealized gains that had been available were eliminated in the sharp market decline, threatening the ability of Japanese banks to comply with the Basel Accord.

The imposition of stricter capital standards has prompted U.S. banks to respond by raising capital in the stock and bond markets, especially the large money center banks that have consistently operated with lower capital ratios than smaller regional banks. In 1992, total bank issuances amounted to $46 billion, with stock representing $10 billion and debt $36 billion. This topped the 1991 record of $29 billion in total offerings. The $1.2 billion common stock issue of Chemical Banking ranked as the largest bank issue and the fourth largest overall corporate issue for 1992.

The structural differences in the United States and Japan create a different environment for the response of banks in raising capital, however. The major Japanese banks, the *city banks*, are members of Japanese *keiretsu*. As much as 80 percent of stock of these firms is owned by other firms in the group--commercial and industrial firms. Since the mid-1980s, between 60 and 90 percent of all new common stock issued by Japanese banks has been purchased by other keiretsu members. In addition, the banks have raised funds through subordinated bonds issued through offshore subsidiaries and subordinated loans borrowed primarily from domestic life insurance companies, generally members of their own *keiretsu*.

This difference in the U.S. and Japanese systems goes well beyond the issue of adequate capital levels. In fact, there are significant differences in the regulatory environment of banks in the United States and those in other countries. These differences help to explain the major influence of foreign banks in the United States. The dynamics of the relationship between the banking industry and its regulators have far-reaching impact.

The United States

For historical reasons, in the United States, the relationship between government and business has been a somewhat arms-length arrangement. This appears to be attributable to two primary factors. First, large concentrations of financial power have never been readily accepted, as evidenced by an extensive body of antitrust law and court cases. Secondly, strong emphasis on public disclosure of government activity has produced "sunshine" and freedom-of-information laws.

These factors have made it difficult for commercial banks and government officials in the United States to develop extremely close working relationships. From the banks's perspective, the loss of confidentiality that would accompany a closer relationship with government could be a disadvantage, particularly, if the bank sought greater market share or contemplated a politically unfavorable (albeit completely legal) strategy.

As a result of these factors, the relationship between U.S. banks and government may be accurately characterized as adversarial. The focus of U.S. legislation has been geared more towards protecting consumers and less towards reviewing policies to ensure the international competitiveness of U.S. banks.

Active Consumer Protection

In 1968, the *Consumer Credit Protection Act* was passed. This multi-faceted law was quite explicit in protecting the rights of consumers from any misconduct on the part of banks in their consumer banking activities. The primary legislation was contained in seven different sections of the act:

- *Truth-in-Lending Act (TILA)*--effective July 1969. TILA is designed to ensure that consumers more easily understand the terms of credit and avoid the uninformed use of credit.
- *Fair Credit Billing Act (FCBA)*--effective October 1975. FCBA addresses the resolution of billing errors in connection with credit card accounts.

- *Consumer Leasing Act (CLA)*--effective March 1977. CLA essentially covers the same type of disclosure as for loans (TILA) in the area of consumer leases of personal property for personal, family, or household use.
- *Fair Credit Reporting Act (FCRA)*--effective April 1971. FCRA regulates consumer reporting by placing disclosure obligations on users of credit reports; requiring fair, timely, and accurate reporting of credit information; restricting use of credit reports; and requiring deletion of obsolete information.
- *Fair Credit Opportunity Act (FCOA)*--effective October 1975. FCOA prohibits treating any applicant or group of applicants less favorably than others on the basis of race, color, religion, national origin, sex, marital status, age, or receipt of income from public assistance sources.
- *Fair Debt Collection Practices Act (FDCPA)*--effective March 1978. FDCPA is intended to protect consumers from abusive, deceptive, and unfair debt collection practices.
- *Electronic Fund Transfers Act (EFTA)*--fully effective May 1980. EFTA establishes the rights and responsibilities of participants in electronic funds transfer systems.

Enforcement of most of these acts is effected through Federal Reserve regulations. In addition to these provisions of the Consumer Credit Protection Act, other laws have been enacted that govern the consumer banking. *The Fair Housing Act* (a component of the Civil Rights Act of 1968) has been interpreted by the courts to prohibit lending institutions from such practices as redlining (denying mortgage loans in certain areas even though applicants otherwise qualify), making excessively low property appraisal values in the case of minority applicants (forcing higher down payments), or establishing excessively burdensome qualification standards for minority applicants.

The *Community Reinvestment Act (CRA)* of 1977 is another significant consumer protection law. It requires federal regulators (Comptroller, Federal Reserve, and FDIC) to encourage the banks they oversee to provide for the credit needs of the communities they serve.[19] The law mandates that regulators assess an institution's record of providing for

19. Similar provisions apply for savings and loan associations.

the credit needs of the entire community, including low- and moderate-income neighborhoods. This record is to be considered when a bank seeks a new charter, acquires shares of another bank, or merges with another bank.

The objective of the CRA is to discourage the practice of redlining. If banks wish to expand, this legislation requires that they demonstrate that they are not neglecting under-served, disadvantaged areas, although if a bank is not located to serve such an area, the law has virtually no effect on it.

The Financial Institutions Reform, Recovery, and Enforcement Act of 1989 (FIRREA) strengthened the 1977 law by requiring that regulators regularly prepare a written evaluation of each bank's community reinvestment. A portion of this evaluation that must now be made public includes the institution's rating:

- outstanding
- satisfactory
- needs to improve
- substantial noncompliance

The documentation for the rating must also be made public.

Other laws which impact consumer banking practices include:

- The Real Estate Settlement Procedures Act of 1974, requiring relevant and timely disclosures as to the nature and cost of the real estate settlement process.
- The Expedited Funds Availability Act (a component of the Competitive Equality Banking Act of 1987), placing restrictions on the length of time that a bank may deny funds availability after a customer deposits checks.
- The Bank Secrecy Act of 1970 and its 1986 amendment contained in the Money Laundering Control Act of 1986, requiring banks to report deposit, withdrawal, or other exchange of currency in the amount of $10,000 or more.
- The Right to Financial Privacy Act of 1978, prohibiting the disclosure of customer information to federal authorities in the absence of specific documentation.
- The Truth in Savings Act of 1987, requiring full disclosure of interest rate, fees, minimum balances, term, and penalties for all demand or interest-bearing accounts.

As illustrated by this partial list of laws that cover consumer banking, the government has been quite focused on the protection of consumer rights. While such protection is clearly warranted, some have also argued that the burden of compliance has become excessive. It has been estimated that the U.S. banking industry spends $11 billion annually to comply with bank regulations--fully a third of the industry's net income for 1992.

Benign Neglect of the Banks

At the same time, U.S. lawmakers have been less consistent in their attention to necessary legislative remedies to make the banking system more internationally competitive. Federal bank regulation has limited the natural expansion of the banking system almost from the outset. From 1933 to 1978 this regulation was particularly restrictive. Since that time, the remedies that have been afforded only partially address the issue of international competitiveness.

The National Bank Act of 1863 created a banking organization that would be chartered under federal law by the Office of the Comptroller of the Currency. The national bank would not repeat the "mistakes" of the First Bank of the United States (1791-1811) or of the Second Bank of the United States (1816-1836). These earlier federal banks had branched nationwide, had infringed on the perceived territorial rights of state-chartered banks, and (as a direct result) had not been granted renewal of their 20-year charters.

Because the earlier banks had been so unpopular with certain powerful political forces, the geographic scope of national banks was restricted to one location. Thus, national banks were originally unit banks with no branches, rendering them less threatening and more readily accepted. Meanwhile, state banks were granted a much wider geographic scope of operation and given less restrictive guidelines as to capital, lending, and liquidity requirements. State bank charters offered many advantages not shared by national banks. At the same time, national banks were expected to help solidify the banking system and the currency by issuing bank notes (bank liabilities convertible into gold or silver) that were uniform regardless of the state in which they operated.

Such contradictions in policy did not address the need for a strong, unified national banking system. Instead, a *dual-banking* system developed, with banks chartered by both state banking authorities and the Comptroller of the Currency. This is an early example of the lack of a comprehensive, coherent policy to address the banking needs of the country.

After persistent money panics continued to occur, the Federal Reserve Act of 1913 created a central banking mechanism with 12 districts presumably to address the problems of the fragmented banking system that had evolved. (By 1920, there were over 30,000 banks in the United States--with both state and national charters.) The Federal Reserve Act also began to loosen the restrictions on national banks. Up to this time, only state banks and private, nonincorporated banks were permitted to establish foreign branches. Essentially, there had not been much interest in international operations before World War I because Great Britain was the primary exporter of capital and had assumed the role of world banker.

Around the turn of the century, industry in the United States grew and, along with it, U.S. exports. In 1860 the U.S. trade surplus (exports in excess of imports) was $38 million; by 1920, it had increased to almost $3 billion. In 1913, there were only six state-chartered banking organizations that engaged in overseas banking. The Federal Reserve Act gave national banks permission to establish foreign branches by obtaining permission from the Comptroller of the Currency. To qualify, a bank was required to have $1 million in capital and to agree to full disclosure with respect to foreign branch operations.

Edge Act and Agreement Corporations

A 1916 amendment of the Federal Reserve Act empowered national banks (with $1 million in capital) to invest up to 10 percent of capital in state-chartered banks or corporations that were engaged primarily in international banking. These *Agreement corporations* agree to be subject to limitations and restrictions imposed by the Federal Reserve Board.

Another amendment of the Federal Reserve Act in 1919 created *Edge Act corporations* that are federally chartered institutions for foreign transactions. An added advantage of Edge Act Corporations is that they may invest in nonbank financial institutions, a privilege not explicitly granted to Agreement corporations.

The McFadden Act

With these laws, federal legislators exhibited an interest in encouraging the international competitiveness of U.S. banks. This intent is further evidenced by enactment of the McFadden Act of 1927 which gave national banks the ability to branch within their home states to the extent allowed by state law. National banks were no longer required to maintain a unit banking structure. The McFadden legislation thus represented a kind of liberation of the national banking system. However, in the context of today's banking environment, the McFadden Act is much more restrictive than the laws that govern branching in other countries. The conditions under which U.S. banks must compete has changed dramatically, but federal law with respect to branching has not.

The Glass-Steagall Act

The Banking Act of 1933, often referred to as the Glass-Steagall Act, represented a significant shift in legislative attitude toward the U.S. banking system. The commercial banking industry was stripped of the ability to meaningfully participate in long-term financing of corporate America. Before the Stock Market Crash of 1929, major U.S. banks frequently engaged in both short-term and long-term financing. However, the banks were accused of conflict of interest--promoting questionable securities and then selling them to their deposit clients and trust accounts. The two types of activities would be separated and commercial banking made safer.

The Federal Deposit Insurance Corporation was created to give depositors confidence in the new, more narrowly focused banking system. Interest paid on demand deposits was prohibited; interest paid on savings and time deposits was regulated. Moreover, no institution that engaged in securities transactions could issue deposits. Thus, commercial banks received a bank-financed insurance program and a steady source of low-cost funds.

Bank failures on the scale that had been experienced would hopefully be averted in the future. From a high of 30,000 banks in 1920, the number of U.S. banks plummeted to 15,000 by 1933. From 1929 to early 1933, the money supply shrank by more than one-third. The crisis had not been contained by the Federal Reserve. In fact, the country's banking problems were exacerbated by Federal Reserve actions. The Fed engaged in open-market operations to purchase securities and increase the money supply in 1932 for only a brief period of time. Beginning in April, the Fed bought as much as $100 million in government securities per week. When the effort abruptly ended in early summer, massive bank failures soon resumed. As a result of the Depression and the accompanying banking crisis, the Federal Reserve was reorganized to give more power to the Federal Reserve Board of Governors in Washington.[20] The Federal Open Market Committee was established to set government monetary policy.

While the Federal Reserve was reorganized in the aftermath of the crisis, the commercial banking system was effectively punished. Exclusive rights to issue deposit instruments, interest-rate ceilings, and deposit insurance were exchanged for the ability to compete in the long-term financing of corporate clients. This was an inappropriate response to the problems of the 1930s. The Depression and massive bank failures occurred as a result of depressed prices, accompanying business failures, and a contracted money supply--not because commercial banks underwrote corporate stocks and bonds. To make matters worse, foreign banks with U.S. affiliates were not affected by the Glass-Steagall reforms. This was a significant turning point in the relationship between the banking industry and the U.S. legislature. It marked the beginning of a period of neglect of the competitive needs of the banking system.

Growth of International Banking

Ironically, the industrial production associated with World War II (1939-1945) helped to revitalize the U.S. economy to a great extent. As a result, the vulnerability of the banking system that had been legislated in 1933 was not immediately apparent. After the war, the United States enjoyed a competitive advantage in that it supplied the capital and the goods to rebuild much of Europe through the $12 billion Marshall Plan. As European economies recovered and U.S. demand for goods (pent-up by wartime restrictions) expanded, international trade expanded. U.S. companies established overseas operations and the Eurodollar market developed.[21]

As U.S. banks sought to participate in the Eurodollar market, foreign banks also entered the United States when foreign companies also established U.S. operations. Because these foreign banks were not subject to Glass-Steagall, they were not limited in scope of activities. Nor were they limited to geographic expansion in one state by provisions of the McFadden Act. Foreign banks frequently operated their U.S. affiliates under the laws of applicable states. Under these laws, they could cross state lines, engage in

20. The reorganization of the Federal Reserve was accomplished through legislation in 1935.

21. See Chapter 3 for a description of the development of the Eurodollar markets.

nonbanking activities, maintain lower capital levels than national banks, avoid federal reserve requirements and interest rate ceilings, and decline federal deposit insurance. The vulnerabilities of federal bank legislation were becoming more apparent.

The Bank Holding Company Act

U.S. banks reacted by forming bank holding companies that obeyed the letter, if not the spirit, of federal regulation. Bank holding companies enabled banks to operate across state lines and to engage in nonbank activities. The 1933 Banking Act had made some provision for the regulation of bank holding companies, but had essentially left them free to compete in other lines of commerce. Moreover, under the 1993 act, if the existing bank holding companies already had interstate activities, these were exempted from federal regulation, that is, they were grandfathered.

Federal legislators again exhibited a restrictive attitude toward U.S. banks by enacting the Bank Holding Company Act of 1956. There were several motivations for this legislation:

- There was a fear of financial concentration that would result from a few multistate bank holding companies controlling a large share of the banking assets of the United States.
- If major non-financial corporations were affiliated with commercial banks, these firms could dominate the U.S. economy.
- It was felt that the banking should not be exposed to undue risk. If a particular activity was considered unsafe for a commercial bank, it should also be considered unsafe for a bank holding company.
- There was a concern that non-financial firms that were affiliated with a bank would have an unfair advantage over those that firms that did not with respect to preferential financing arrangements.

The Bank Holding Company Act required that holding companies that owned more than one commercial bank divest of those activities that could not be classified as "closely related" to banking. The 1966 Douglas Amendment to the Bank Holding Company Act restricted the ability of bank holding companies from acquiring institutions in other states by prohibiting such acquisitions unless specifically authorized by the laws of the state of the bank being acquired.

U.S. banks were forced to find the loopholes in federal regulation in order to expand and diversify. One such loophole was the one-bank holding company--not subject to federal regulation. Typically, this form of business organization involved a small commercial bank with one or several other nonbank businesses, frequently including insurance. However, there were a few one-bank holding companies that represented more prominent industrial firms. These latter companies were clear examples of the combination of banking and commerce that Congress had sought to avoid. And their numbers increased dramatically--from 117 in 1955 to 783 in 1968. It was found in a study of 684 of the one-bank holding companies that 578 conducted 20 different *financial* nonbank activities and that 397 were involved in 99 different *nonfinancial* nonbank activities.

Such combinations proliferated because of natural synergies. These synergies had been observed in the United States before Glass-Steagall and can still be observed in Japanese keiretsus. However, the U.S. legislature chose to further restrict the banking industry. In a 1970 amendment of the Bank Holding Company Act, Congress extended the regulations to one-bank holding companies. Any impermissible activities begun after June 1968 were to be divested within 10 years. Those begun before this date were grandfathered on the condition that the Federal Reserve review the grandfathered status of nonbanking activities for bank holding companies with assets in excess of $60 million.

Certain activities have been exempted from provisions of the Bank Holding Company Act. Currently, holding companies can own:

- Shares in an investment company which is not a bank holding company and which is not engaged in any business other than investing in securities.
- Shares of any company which is an export trading company.[22]
- Up to 5 percent of any company, including nonfinancial firms.[23]

---

22. An export trading company (ETC) is a trading organization that supplies support services required for export trade. A business is qualified as an ETC if over 50 percent of revenues are derived from the export of goods or services. The Export Trading Company Act of 1982 gave bank holding companies and Edge Act corporations the right to acquire, partially or wholly, ETCs through equity investment. The objective of the legislation was to support U.S. exports.

23. The Bank Merger Act of 1966 established the ranges of stock ownership that govern the Federal Reserve in determining what is considered control by a bank holding company. Up to 4.9 percent of the voting shares does not constitute control and a bank holding company may own up to this percentage without Fed approval. Between 5 and 24.9 percent, the Federal Reserve has discretion to determine whether control exists. At or above 25 percent, control is assumed to exist.

Notably, foreign banks were also exempted from the 1970 amendment of the Bank Holding Company Act. Foreign banks in the United States continued to enjoy a full range of privileges not available to U.S. banks.

Regulation K

The restrictions on U.S. banks were partially relieved by a 1962 amendment of the Federal Reserve Act which allowed U.S. national banks to participate in activities on foreign soil that were classified as impermissible if conducted on domestic soil. Regulation K (which governed the international operations of national banks) was amended to include a statement of national purpose with respect to U.S. bank competitiveness overseas.[24]

"The Congress, in enacting section 25(a) of the Act, provided for the establishment of international banking and financial corporations operating under Federal supervision with powers sufficiently broad to enable them to compete effectively with similar foreign-owned institutions and to afford to the United States exporter and importer in particular--and to United States commerce, industry, and agriculture in general--at all times a means of financing international trade."

"In light of the purposes involved, Corporations should be able in their activities abroad to operate, as best meets their corporate policies, through branches, agencies, and correspondents or through direct and indirect ownership in foreign-chartered companies engaged in banking or other international or foreign operations so as their credit and other activities are in the interest of the United States."

This was recognition of the need for U.S. banks to be internationally competitive overseas. The permissible activities for overseas affiliates includes commercial banking and finance, leasing as functional equivalent of an extension of credit; providing investment advisory services; operating a general insurance agency; managing a mutual fund; providing management consulting services; operating a travel agency in connection with financial services offered abroad; and underwriting, distributing, and dealing in debt and equity securities with certain dollar limits. In some cases, banks have also been permitted to underwrite insurance in other countries.

---

24. See Baker and Bradford, p. 137.

The dollar limits that are imposed on national banks with respect to their securities operations can be quite restrictive, however. No foreign affiliate may underwrite more than $2 million and total underwritings for all subsidiaries may not exceed $15 million. Such low underwriting limits make it exceedingly difficult for U.S. banks to become lead managers, that is, major participants, in large public offerings overseas. In addition, a foreign affiliate of a U.S. bank may underwrite no more than 20 percent of the equity of a commercial firm.

Moreover, until the Fed approval of Section 20 subsidiaries in 1989, no U.S. bank was permitted to participate in *any* corporate securities underwriting domestically. For the years that elapsed between 1933 and 1978, foreign banks had a clear advantage over domestic banks in the United States. Foreign banks were not subject to the provisions of Glass-Steagall or the Bank Holding Company Act.

International Banking Act

It was not until enactment of the International Banking Act in 1978 that the playing field for U.S. banks was at least partially leveled. The act does not directly make foreign banks subject to Glass-Steagall, but instead, takes the approach of making them bank holding companies. As such, foreign banks must adhere to the list of permissible nonbank activities. Since corporate securities underwriting is not on this list, the act effectively precluded their participation in this activity. However, the securities subsidiaries of the 17 foreign banks that already existed were grandfathered. In addition, any foreign affiliate operating as a federal branch was required to be insured by FDIC if it accepted deposits in amounts less than $100,000.

The International Banking Act placed U.S. banks on more equal footing but it did not remove the advantages that foreign banks had accrued in the United States during the period from 1933 to 1978. Nor did it address the restricted activities of U.S. banks overseas vis-à-vis their counterparts from other countries.

The FDIC Improvement Act of 1991

Provisions of the FDICIA, among other things, attempted to lessen the differences in operational freedom among domestic nationally chartered banks, state banks, and foreign banks.[25] Instead of giving greater freedoms to national banks, however, it reduced the scope of activity for the other two categories. The act restricts state banks' ability to:

- Own and develop real estate.
- Underwrite securities.
- Act as real estate brokers.
- Sell or underwrite insurance.

FDICIA limits a state bank's insurance underwriting and equity investments to those allowed for national banks. If a state bank wishes to act as principal in nonpermissible activities, it must comply with all capital standards and have a written determination from FDIC that the activity poses no significant threat to the deposit insurance fund. Those banks that underwrite insurance in Delaware are grandfathered with respect to any underwriting engaged in before November 1991. Savings banks in New York and New England also may continue to offer life insurance.

State-licensed branches or agencies of foreign banks are subject to similar provisions. Specifically, the Fed may approve nonpermissible activities if it finds that the activity is consistent with sound banking practices. Additionally, if a foreign branch is insured, the FDIC must find that the activity poses no significant risk to the insurance fund.

An Appeal to Government

In this environment of tightening regulations, the banking industry has appealed to the U.S. government for specific relief. Six major bank trade associations--the American Bankers Association, the Association of Reserve City Bankers, the Consumer Bankers Association, the Independent Bankers Association of America, the Association of Bank Holding Companies, and the Savings and Community Bankers of America--formally have asked U.S. President Bill Clinton to eliminate those requirements that restrict lending and impede economic growth and job-creation. Among their recommendations are:

- Repeal certain provisions of the Federal Deposit Insurance Corporation Improvement Act that significantly increase the cost of compliance.

---

25. The FDICIA also addresses deposit insurance assessments. See Chapter 3 for a discussion of these provisions.

- Eliminate market value accounting.
- Use incentives instead of penalties to encourage lending in economically depressed communities.
- Reduce the frequency of regulatory examinations.
- Reduce maximum financial penalties on bank officers.

These requests reflect the frustration felt by the U.S. banking community. The general feeling appears to be that there is too much regulation and that it chokes the ability of commercial banks to adequate serve their clientele.

In the context of the legislative structure of the U.S. banking system, the adversarial nature of the relationship between U.S. banks and their legislators becomes clear. The regulatory process perhaps is viewed as one which imposes restrictions that leave the banks openly vulnerable to competitive forces that they cannot effectively counteract. This natural tension between bankers and regulators is not as readily apparent in other countries.

The United Kingdom

The United States has three federal bank regulators--the Comptroller of the Currency (national banks), the Federal Reserve (bank holding companies and state-chartered members of the Fed), and the Federal Deposit Insurance Corporation (insured banks and state-chartered nonmembers of the Fed). In addition, there are 50 state banking authorities. In contrast, most of the other G-10 have only one chief bank regulator.[26] This makes coordinating and implementing regulatory policies much less complicated. Even when there are regulators along functional lines, for example, a banking regulator and a securities regulator, one is designated as the "lead regulator" to streamline the process. Implementation is also made more efficient by the existence of a few large banks in these countries, as compared to thousands of banks in the United States.

---

26. The Group of Ten, also called G-10, is a group of major industrialized countries that coordinate monetary and fiscal policies. The member are Belgium, Canada, France, Germany, Italy, Japan, the Netherlands, Sweden, the United Kingdom, and the United States. Switzerland is an associate member.

In the case of the United Kingdom, the primary bank regulator was the central bank, the Bank of England. The role of the Bank evolved over time and is characterized by a tradition of "gentlemen's agreements" between it and other British banks. There is no equivalent of the Glass-Steagall Act in the United Kingdom. Until recently, specialized financial institutions engaged in narrowly focused activities because of tradition, not regulation. The U.K. financial system developed with relatively few regulatory guidelines. Originally, the Bank of England was given special privileges in exchange for its financial services to the government. U.K. clearing (commercial) and merchant banks are expected to obtain the concurrence of the Bank of England before taking any significant action.

Recently, the United Kingdom has moved away from this informal system and toward a more structured one. Reasons for this trend are:

- Required harmonization of banking regulations in accordance with European Community directives.
- Changes in the structure of the City (London's financial district) caused by the Big Bang of 1986 which accelerated the move toward broad-based, diversified financial institutions.
- Growth in the number of firms operating in the City.
- The failures of several financial institutions.

In 1974, several smaller institutions failed and the Bank of England organized a "lifeboat" rescue to maintain liquidity in the system. The 1979 Banking Act formalized the role of the Bank of England as supervisor of the banking system and required all deposit taking institutions to be licensed by the Bank. When Johnson Matthey Bankers failed in 1984, concerns were raised once again as to the adequacy of bank regulation. The Banking Act of 1987 further strengthened the powers of the Bank of England. Nevertheless, the U.K. central bank continues to exhibit a preference for informal approaches to bank supervision and regulation.

There is a higher degree of informality and flexibility in the U.K. system relative to the U.S. system. The Bank of England does not conduct on-site examinations of banks, but instead relies on regularly filed, detailed statistical reports and on meetings with management. The Bank also uses private audit reports. This approach makes it possible to review each institution on a case-by-case basis. There is little need for extensive regulations to govern each aspect of banking.

When financial institutions acquire other firms or engage in new activities in the United Kingdom, they need not make formal application.

Instead, it is only necessary to seek the approval of the Bank of England on an informal basis. The Bank has considerable influence in this informal process and a financial firm is unlikely to act against the advice of the Bank.

Clearing banks have always been permitted to engage in securities activities and there are no formal restrictions on the relationship between banks and nonfinancial firms. Although not required to do so, most banks conduct their securities activities through separate subsidiaries. Also, banks may extend credit to their securities subsidiaries as long as such credit is made available in accordance with prudent banking practice and within those guidelines established by the Bank of England.

British banks may engage in almost any type of financial activity. Three exceptions to this general rule are also permitted but must be conducted in separated capitalized subsidiaries:

- Government securities dealings.
- Life assurance (insurance) activities.
- Management of a unit trust (mutual fund).

In this way, clearing banks have been permitted to develop into diversified financial services groups that engage in universal banking.

The Financial Services Act of 1987 created an elaborate system of authorization, regulation, and supervision. Under this act, the Department of Trade and Industry (DTI) was given the responsibility to regulate U.K. securities industry. DTI delegated responsibilities for securities regulation to the newly formed Securities and Investments Board (SIB), which it oversees. The SIB is functionally similar to the U.S. Securities and Exchange Commission (SEC) except that it is a private organization, financed by fees of its members. Self Regulatory Organizations (SROs) set the standards of conduct and practice for their members.

The Financial Services Act requires that any firm that engages in "investment activities" be authorized by either the SIB or by its SRO. Investment activities include providing investment advice and the sale or management of:

- equity shares
- corporate bonds
- government and local bonds
- depository receipts
- warrants
- units in a unit investment trust
- options and futures

The SROs that cover various investment activities are:

- Securities Association
- Investment Management Regulatory Organization
- Association of Futures Brokers and Dealers
- Financial Intermediaries Managers
- Brokers Regulatory Association
- Life Assurance and Unit Trust Regulatory Organization

Since British banks perform a number of financial services, they must be members of each applicable SRO. This is considered *functional* regulation, that is, regulation by type of activity. To reduce duplication of effort, however, each type of institution has a "lead regulator," which designation depends on the primary function of the financial institution. For a banking group, the Bank of England is lead regulator and sets requirements for the firm as a whole. The various SROs are responsible for the firm's compliance only in their functional areas.

In terms of nonfinancial activities, there are no legal barriers between banking and industry. Traditionally, however, the Bank of England has indicated that proposals for a combination of banking and industrial/commercial firms would be subject to close scrutiny because of the concentrated nature of banking in the United Kingdom. Commercial banks do own merchant banks that, in turn, own equity in nonfinancial, commercial and industrial firms. The reverse is not observed--merchant banks do not own commercial banks. Moreover, it is not anticipated that commercial banks will become direct owners of large amounts of industrial equities.

Nevertheless, the full range of financial services is open to British banks. The relationship between the banks and their regulators is based on a kind of mutual respect that transcends rules and regulations. Part of this phenomenon is attributable to common background and experience, particularly with respect to the Conservative Party in the government. Beginning in the 1960s, young members of the Tory party often were invited to spend several years working in the City--providing them with insight into the financial community and perhaps instilling a certain amount of loyalty to the firms operating there. In addition, the case-by-case style of regulation in the United Kingdom makes it easier to avoid offensive or defensive positions that can be encouraged by a extensive amount of written rules. Potential problems are more quickly addressed and the financial system is not exposed to decades of overly restrictive regulation. This is particularly true now that the Financial Services Authority has been formed to coordinate the regulation of the banking, insurance, and securities industries.

Germany

The Banking Act of 1961 defines banking business in Germany. The specified activities include:

- Deposit taking.
- Consumer and industrial lending.
- Trading (for the account of others) government debt instruments and corporate debt and equity securities.
- Operating a mutual fund.
- Custodial securities business.

Any firm that is engaged in banking business is considered a bank and must be licensed and supervised by the Federal Banking Supervisory Office and the Bundesbank (central bank). In addition to the activities specified in the Banking Act, banks offer other services, within the bank itself:

Underwriting and dealing in government and corporate debt and equity instruments.

- Investment advice.
- Management consulting.
- Factoring.
- Leasing.
- Real estate brokerage and investment.

These functions are performed in departments within the bank, not in separate subsidiaries. The separation between commercial and investment banking that is observed in the United States does not exist in Germany. Moreover, the structure of subsidiaries to separate the functions within a banking group, as in the United Kingdom, is not used. In fact, it is felt that using such "firewalls" only constrains the flow of funds within the bank.

The subsidiary structure is required in German for the following lines of business:

- Insurance.
- Investment fund (mutual fund).
- Issuance of mortgage-backed bonds and municipal bonds backed by loans to municipalities.

- Transactions of building and loan associations.

German banks can be classified by legal form and ownership: commercial banks (including the Big Three--Deutsche Bank, Dresdner Bank, and Commerzbank--and regional banks), savings banks (with municipal, regional, or state authorities providing capital), cooperative banks (with members providing capital), and specialized banks (including mortgage banks and building and loan associations). Regardless of legal structure, approximately 95 percent of German banks can engage in universal banking. Historically, many have elected to specialize in particular lines of business. More recently, however, competitive pressures have resulted in an expansion of services offered.

In terms of regulation, the Bundesbank acts primarily to collect data from the banks in a network of regional and local offices. The primary regulatory responsibility rests with the Federal Banking Supervisory Office (FBSO). The FBSO regulates the activities of all forms of German banks. In this role, the agency has a broad range of powers including information gathering, investigation, and intervention. It is also within the purview of the FBSO to determine appropriate levels of capital and liquidity, relying less on routine on-site examinations and more on annual external audits, detailed periodic reports, and special investigations.

As is true in the case of U.K. bank regulation, German regulation is less adversarial. Like their U.S. counterparts, professional banking associations have formed to represent the interests of their members. Unlike the U.S. case, however, the German government is required by law to consult with these banking associations when new or amended banking regulations are being considered. This arrangement gives banking associations a semi-official status.

This relationship between banking and government has not gone without challenge and strong debate about the role of universal banks. The issue has been whether these banks, particularly the Big Three which own a large share of German industrial stocks, wield too much power. In 1979, the Gessler Commission, among other things, examined whether banks faced a conflict of interest. Did their close relationships with clients provide them with insider information that gave them an unfair advantage in equity markets? In their findings the Commission endorsed the present system and did not conclude that German banks had excessive control over German industry. The Commission did recommend, however, that banks limit their equity holdings to 25 percent of the equity capital of a particular firm.

Recently, the German Monopolies Commission recommended that equity participations be limited to 5 percent of bank capital.

Over the last decade, German banks have substantially reduced their stock investments in nonfinancial firms. It is notable that this has been accomplished without the force of law and without stripping German banks of their universal banking powers. The relationships between banks and government works well in that the objectives of both sectors appear to be largely accomplished through consultation and negotiation.

Another example of this working relationship involves the German export sector which consistently has been the key to German economic viability. The banks have generally conducted international business in a way that was consistent with the government's foreign policy interests. An effective way to elicit commercial bank support of overseas trade has been the *government guarantee* of loans for international trade. These guarantees signal official desires, without resorting to directives. *Moral suasion* and implied *futures government assistance* (as needed) have also been used.

Standard guarantees, for exports and raw materials, available on a fee basis, help to both stimulate the export sector and to assure adequate quantities of raw materials necessary for the industrial sector. Most individual transactions have little or no impact on foreign policy. Thus, the *Hermes guarantee*, as such a guarantee is called, is important to a German bank only if the financial risk of the underlying international loan exceeds the bank's comfort level.

In some cases, however, specific transactions have considerable significance for foreign policy. In those situations, *exceptional guarantees* may be issued. The standard Hermes guarantees cover from 85% of the loan (in the case of a German export) to 95% (in the case of a German import). In exceptional circumstances, insurance coverage is reduced or increased.

For example, in 1976, the potential sale of nuclear reactors to Brazil had significant consequences for the German nuclear energy sector. At the time, the domestic market was saturated, with only 70% utilization of nuclear power plant manufacturing facilities. The government had invested \$5 billion in research and development. Up to 13,000 domestic jobs were at stake. Further, if the transaction were completed, the government would be in a much better position to obtain long-term supplies of uranium from deposits in Brazil.

The Hermes guarantee associated with the sale of these reactors covered 95% of the loan, rather than the customary 85%. The term of the guarantee was 20 years, an unusually long period of time for an export/import transaction. In this case, the government worked with the banking industry to bring about a desirable outcome for the entire German economy.

More recently, the banking system worked in close partnership with the government to ease the monetary transition of the reunification of East and West Germany. In April 1990, the ostmarks of the East Germany were to be converted to deutsche marks. Without such as conversion, in advance of formal reunification, it would have been extremely difficult for the German government to stem the flow of East Germans to the West. This involved providing 16.5 million East Germans with cash in two days, exchanging deutsche marks for ostmarks on a one-for-one basis (using bank accounts as well as notes and coin) and converting 28 million savings and checking accounts on July 1 from ostmarks to deutsche marks.

In 1989, when it became clear that, in the future, West German banks would be permitted to operate once again in East Germany, Deutsche Bank began to give crash courses in banking to the staff of East German banks. Managers were taught the basics of the West German social market economy during weekend seminars. East German bankers learned the modern technology of electronic funds transfer. Other West German banks joined the crusade to update the East German system. In the process, Deutsche Bank, Dresdner Bank, and Commerzbank have collectively opened over 300 new offices. Each of the Big Three has already spent or plans to spend up to DM1 billion in acquisitions and start-up costs in eastern Germany. It is clear that the banking system played a critical role in those early days of German reunification. It is equally clear that the relationship between the German government and banking sectors is typically one of mutual support.

Japan

The Japanese regulatory structure for banks is even more streamlined than the German. The Ministry of Finance is the principal regulator of the entire Japanese financial system. It is made up of seven bureaus: Budget (government expenditures), Tax (government revenue), Finance (government debt), Customs (customs revenue), Banking (banking sector), Securities (securities sector), International Finance (foreign operations of

Japanese financial institutions). With the exception of the minister and two vice-ministers, the Ministry of Finance is composed of bureaucrats that typically spend their entire 30-year careers with the Ministry. While there is potential for conflict between the bureaus, most personnel rotate assignments within the Ministry, generally every two years. This enhances the amount of cooperation and coordination between the bureaus.

The Ministry of Finance is thus one unified regulator with duties that parallel a number of U.S. agencies--the Federal Reserve Board, the Office of the Comptroller of the Currency, the Federal Deposit Insurance Corporation, the Office of Thrift Supervision, the Securities and Exchange Commission, the Commodities Future Trading Corporation, and the U.S. Treasury (including the Internal Revenue Service).

The Bank of Japan (central bank) is under the direction of the Ministry of Finance. The Bank also exerts control over commercial banks because it lends funds to Japanese banks to a much greater extent than U.S. banks are permitted to borrow from the Federal Reserve. Also, the Bank monitors bank positions and uses "window guidance" to tell banks what it feels is appropriate with respect to lending policy. While banks are not required to comply with these suggestions, the Bank's control over credit markets ensures compliance.

While this system appears to offer the banks have very little input into the process of regulation and operation, the relationship between Japanese banks and regulators is characterized by negotiation. For example, in 1965 the Diet (federal legislature) was faced with an economic recession. Together the Diet and the Ministry of Finance constructed a plan for deficit spending to spur the economy. A Government Bond Syndicate was formed in the fall of 1965 that would function as an alternative to the open market issuance of government bonds. Leaders of the banking community worked with members of the Debt Division of the Finance Bureau. Together, they agreed upon a mutually acceptable bond issue for the entire year. Each month the Syndicate purchased the allocation and one year later the bonds were repurchased by the government at par.

The banks agreed not to deal in bonds, as this was the right of securities firms. Over time, bank holdings of government bonds grew--to ¥4.5 trillion in 1975, ¥11 trillion in 1977, and then ¥18.4 trillion in 1978--and the government grew less willing to buy back large quantities for fear of the inflationary effects. Understandably, the banks sought the right to trade these government bonds. The securities firms (perhaps just as understandably) resisted this infringement on their turf, noting that Article 65 expressly prohibited banks from engaging in securities activities.

Together, the Banking Bureau and the Securities Bureau within the Ministry of Finance reached a compromise. In the Banking Act of 1982, banks were given the ability to sell government bonds over the counter to profit from price fluctuations beginning April 1983 and in the secondary market beginning June 1984. In exchange, securities firms were allowed to lend money to customers using government bonds as collateral. By 1984, the bond market in Japan was second only to that of the United States, with most of the activity in government bonds. Other bank reforms have followed--all the result of compromises between the banking system and the Ministry of Finance.

Essentially, major Japanese banks view matters from a long-term perspective in which their own success is tied to the nation's economic viability. This process of compromise is also apparent in the area of international banking. Japanese banks frequently concentrate on lending and deposit-taking in countries that are major trading partners. Since Japan depends so heavily on imported raw materials and other goods, there are numerous overseas bank locations in resource-rich nations. Frequently, the government has used international lending to offset deficits and surpluses in the country's balance of payments.

In the early 1970s, Japan enjoyed trade surpluses and a buildup of official international reserves (foreign currency). From 1970 to 1973, foreign-currency-denominated loans were permitted for the first time and restrictions on capital export (overseas loans and other investments) were relaxed. The government itself deposited substantial amounts of foreign currency in the banking system which enabled commercial banks to develop a Euroloan portfolio.

From 1973 to 1975, Japanese surpluses turned into deficits as steep crude oil price increases took their toll. The government reacted by restricting medium- and long-term loans to nonresidents denominated in foreign currency. At the same time, incentives to encourage capital inflow (borrowing from overseas sources) were instituted. As the balance of payments has changed from surplus to deficit and then back again, the Japanese government has adjusted the restrictions on international banking accordingly. At times, action has gone beyond even these measures.

In 1980, special incentives were put in place to attract OPEC trade surpluses to Japan. The 5.5% interest rate ceiling on yen deposits was lifted and normal withholding taxes on interest earned on bank deposits were waived for deposits by foreign governments and by international institutions. The Japanese government supplemented these measures with direct diplomatic consultations with Middle Eastern governments. Predictably, foreign deposits rose dramatically. Although implemented in a different way, Japanese government policy with respect to international banking has been as effective as the German.

Technically, the Japanese government (through the Ministry of Finance and the Bank of Japan) wields considerable influence over that country's banking system. In practice, however, it is clear that the government is only as powerful as the economy that it oversees and that the economy depends to a large measure on the banking system and industrial firms. Thus, in considering Japanese government, banking, and industry, it is not appropriate to view the government as dominant or all-powerful, but instead as "first among equals."

Conclusion

The regulation of commercial banks is justified by the same concerns in all industrialized countries. Safety and soundness of the banking system is a critical component of economic viability. From the relatively informal regulatory system of the United Kingdom to the highly regimented system of Japan, there is always a natural tension between the banking industry and its regulators. Nevertheless, the U.S. system presents a sharp contrast to the more negotiated process of compromise that can be observed outside the United States. This a critical difference, whether operating within U.S. boundaries or in a more global setting.

Selected References

Baker, James C. and M. Gerald Bradford. *American Banks Abroad: Edge Act Companies and Multinational Banking*, Praeger Publishers, New York, 1974.

"Bank Financings Hit a Gusher," *United States Banker*, February 1993, pp. 16-21.

Coulbeck, Neil. *The Multinational Banking Industry*, New York University Press, New York, 1984.

Dale, Richard. *The Regulation of International Banking*, Prentice-Hall, Englewood Cliffs, New Jersey, 1986.

Friedland, Jonathan. "Into the Whirlpool: Japan's Banking Crisis Looks Set to Worsen as Loan Losses Mount," *Far Eastern Economic Review*, April 8, 1993, pp. 70-74.

Greider, William. *Secrets of the Temple: How the Federal Reserve Runs the Country*, Touchstone/Simon & Schuster, New York, 1989.

A Guide to the FDIC Improvement Act, Price Waterhouse, March 1992.

Hales, Michael G. *Handbook of Consumer Banking Law*, Prentice Hall, Englewood Cliffs, New Jersey, 1989.

Hilton, Anthony. *City Within a State: A Portrait of Britain's Financial World*, I.B. Tauris & Co., London, 1987.

International Monetary Fund. *International Capital Markets: Developments and Prospects*, Washington, D.C., 1989.

Johnson, Hazel J. *The Bank Valuation Handbook: A Market-Based Approach to Valuing a Bank*. Probus Publishing, Chicago, 1993 and Irwin Professional Publishing, 1995.

Khambata, Dara M. *The Practice of Multinational Banking: Macro-Policy Issues and Key International Concepts*, Quorum Books, New York, 1986.

Lee, Peter. "Banks Lean on Clinton," *Euromoney*, February, 1993, pp. 34-38.

Pecchioli, R. M. *Prudential Supervision in Banking*, Organization for Economic Co-operation and Development, Paris, 1987.

Rosenbluth, Frances McCall. *Financial Politics in Contemporary Japan*, Cornell University Press, Ithaca, New York, 1989.

Shirreff, David. "Can Anyone Tame the Currency Market?" *Euromoney*, September 1993, pp. 60-69.

Spong, Kenneth. *Banking Regulation: Its Purpose, Implementation, and Effects*, 3rd edition, Federal Reserve Bank of Kansas, 1990.

Subcommittee on Financial Institutions Supervision, Regulation, and Insurance. *Report of the Task Force on the International Competitiveness of U.S. Financial Institutions*, Committee on Banking Finance and Urban Affairs, Washington, D.C., 1990.

U.S. Department of the Treasury. *Modernizing the Financial System: Recommendations for Safer, More Competitive Banks*, Washington, D.C., 1991.

Wilson, J.S. *Banking Policy and Structure: A Comparative Analysis*, Croom Helm Ltd., London, 1986.

5. Best Practices

Introduction

Within the context of their respective regulatory environments and the banking systems, the United States, Germany, the United Kingdom, and Japan present interesting contrasts in terms of their comparative advantages. The United States is clearly dominant in the areas of innovation and technology. Germany has mastered the art of corporate relations. The United Kingdom is perhaps the world's most internationalized banking system. Even in the face of recent financial reverses, Japanese banks present a model for coordination and control. As the global banking community becomes more integrated, these advantages will no doubt be exploited.

Innovation in the United States

U.S. banks have been pioneers in bank innovation which has been applied in both corporate and retail markets. Loan sales, asset-backed securities, index CDs, swaps, and mezzanine finance are but a few examples.

Loan Sales

Commercial banks are being transformed from deposit-takers and loan-makers into institutions that offer a wide range of financial services. Money market funds and deregulation have made it impossible for banks to fund themselves at below-market rates on deposits and borrowings. The ability of blue-chip corporate clients to obtain lower-cost financing in the commercial paper market has seriously eroded the traditional loan market. The more "bankable" middle market of corporate America now has access to private placement funding and to below-investment-grade bond issuance.[27] Moreover, overcapacity in the U.S. banking system, the formidable presence of foreign banks, and the growth of nonbank financial institutions have increased competition significantly. At the same time, regulatory restrictions on the scope of activity and geographic dispersion have limited the available responses by commercial banks.

The sale of loans represents one of these responses. The process of originating and then selling loans de-emphasizes the traditional role of deposit-taker and loan-maker and enables a bank to better diversify its portfolio. Moving loans "off the books" also reduces the amount of required capital. When a bank performs these functions, it is considered an originator or seller in this market.

Another bank that is less competitive in terms of originating loans can also participate in attractive loans to which it otherwise might not have access. In this role, the bank is considered an investor in the loan sales market. An investor may be an *assignee*, that is, one with the same rights and responsibilities as the original members of the loan syndicate in the primary market. Alternatively, an investor may be a *participant* whose rights, by market convention, are limited to a vote on amendments that would (1) lower the rate of interest or commitment fees or (2) forgive interest on principal.

The originator in the market must consider relationships with *borrowers*, relationships with *investors*, and *portfolio* management and profitability. In structuring a loan, the originator must be sensitive to competitive conditions with respect to price and terms for the *borrower*. For its part, the borrower is likely to be concerned about the size and sophistication of the lending group, with the original syndicate usually drawn from the borrower's traditional banking group. There is often an implicit understanding that the original and assignee lenders will buy back portions of the credit if the borrower requests a loan agreement amendment that the participating lenders is reluctant to grant. While this has historically

27. It should be noted that legislative restrictions such as the Glass-Steagall Act still prevent small- and medium-sized businesses from obtaining adequate long-term financing. Also, the new risk-based capital standards require higher capital for corporate loans than for Treasury securities or residential mortgage loans. Such laws, regulations, and capital requirements discourage financing in this critical area.

been the case, this implicit understanding may become less prevalent as this market becomes more standardized.

At the same time, the originator also must be aware of features that are important to the *investor* in terms of structure and pricing. In an investment-banking tradition, originators develop a group of loyal assignees and participants that will consider seriously any deal presented by the originating bank. In some cases, an originator uses its specific information about its investors to "source" loans for assignees and participants that may not fit its own lending interests. An originator may even review its existing loan portfolio to identify credits that would appeal to its investors. Besides the loans themselves, investors should feel confidence that the originator is able to handle the operational aspects of the sale, including timely notification of borrowings, repayments, and repricings.

Volatility in credit markets has resulted in some bank managers seeking only those new loans that can be sold in secondary markets, to ensure needed liquidity of the *asset portfolio*. Of course, profitability is also a consideration. When loans are sold and origination fees are collected, both return on assets and return on equity increase. If market conditions warrant, it may also be possible to earn a "skim," that is, the difference between the contract interest rate earned by the original syndicate and that required by the investors. Also, the originator must be sensitive to diversification in terms of location, industry, and type of loan arrangement.

Foreign banks were the first major investors in the loan sales market. Recently, nonbank financial institutions have become more prominent, including insurance companies, pension funds, savings and loan associations, and mutual funds. There is even a short-term equivalent to commercial paper that has attracted a significant number of nonbank investors.

In the mid-1990s, those banks that wrote down their troubled commercial real estate loans to 45 percent of face often realized profit by selling in the secondary market at 55 percent of face. Cash proceeds were reinvested in low-risk Treasuries or even in other real estate related products. For example, Fleet, during its own bulk disposal of real estate loans, bought into a $105 million private placement by Bankers Trust.

The primary buyers of these loans include the property users, syndicates, individuals, and small institutions. Specialty funds are also often interested buyers, notably those run by Morgan Stanley, Goldman Sachs, and international investment manager George Soros.

Asset-Backed Securities

An asset-backed security is a claim against a pool of loans. In this arrangement, the functions of loan originator (discussed above) are split between the original lenders and the issuer of the asset-backed securities. While it is possible for one party to perform both functions, it is not uncommon for an investment banker to act as issuer. This often has been true in the case of bank loan securitization in which legal constraints forced banks, in the absence of a Section 20 subsidiary, to turn over the actual issuance to investment bankers. However, federal regulators have ruled that banks may securitize loans that they have originated or purchased. The investors in asset-backed securities arrangements, buy discreet securities rather than a portion of a loan pool.

Government agencies were the first to securitize loans to create a secondary market for mortgages--Federal National Mortgage Association (Fannie Mae), Federal Home Loan Mortgage Corporation (Freddie Mac), and Government National Mortgage Association (Ginnie Mae). In addition to the more traditional residential mortgage loans, Fannie Mae is expected to begin to purchase "reverse mortgages." These loans, sometimes also referred to as "home equity conversion loans," are particularly attractive for banks in areas with a high senior citizen population or with a high real estate appreciation potential. The typical borrower is 76 years of age, lives alone, has an annual income of approximately $8,000, and owns a home worth $100,000. Under the arrangement, the bank pays a stipend to the homeowner (collateralized by the real estate) until the house is sold, at which time all interest and principal are repaid.

Originally, in the secondary markets, instruments were merely "pass-throughs" that paid investors their proportional share of interest and principal each month. Likewise, the risks of default and prepayment were also passed through to the investor. For many investors, this was an undesirable situation. The next generation of mortgage-related securities was the mortgage-backed bond that paid interest and principal as a normal bond, with more customary semiannual or quarterly payments and without any prepayment or (original mortgage) default risk.

The most advanced of these instruments is the collateralized mortgage obligation (CMO), introduced by Federal Home Loan Mortgage Corporation but now primarily offered by private investment banks. The various "tranches" of a CMO reduce prepayment risk by devoting all principal payments to the first tranche until it is completely repaid, then to the next tranche until it is completely repaid, and so on. Meanwhile, all tranches receive interest payments unless there is a "Z-bond," that is, a tranche structured like a zero-coupon bond. Growth of mortgage-backed securities has been dramatic since their inception during the 1970s.

The asset-backed securities market now extends well beyond residential mortgages. Beginning in the mid-1980s, General Motors Acceptance Corporation began issuing securities backed by automobile loans. First Boston contributed $40 million in capital and formed a separate corporation, Asset-Backed Securities Corporation (ABSC), to purchase $4 billion in loans from GMAC and to issue the securities. The notes were issued in fast-pay, medium-pay, and slow-pay tranches. Investors received limited protection against default risk from GMAC (5 percent) and First Boston (1 percent). Credit Suisse provided a standby letter of credit that insured timely payment of interest and principal. Because of these financial enhancements, the issue received a AAA rating from Standard and Poor's. After this inaugural issue, Chrysler Financial Corporation, Marine Midland Bank, Empire of America, and Western Financial Savings thereafter also became significant issuers.

Securities backed by credit card loans were also issued. Some of the most significant early originating lenders were First Chicago National Bank (now Bank One), Maryland Bank, Sears, Bank of America, and Manufacturers Hanover (before its merger with Chemical).

Asset-backed securities are either *pass-through* or a *pay-through* arrangements. In a pass-through, the loans are sold to a trust. Investors purchase certificates that represent a proportional share of cash flows from the underlying loans. In order to avoid taxation, the trust must passively transfer all cash flows through to investors. In a pay-through, the loans are transferred to a separate corporation. In this case, there are no restrictions on the management of cash flows and payments to investors need not be tied to cash flows from the underlying loans.

The pay-through structure can be used to eliminate prepayment risk for the investor, when the issuer guarantees a fixed prepayment rate. Should prepayments exceed this guaranteed fixed rate, the proceeds can be invested in a guaranteed investment contract (GIC, commonly issued by insurance companies). When prepayments are less than this guaranteed rate, the issuer can draw on a borrowing facility, perhaps a standby letter of credit from a commercial bank.

The credit risk of an asset-backed security is not tied to the credit risk of the originating lender. The rating agencies (typically Moody's Investor Service and Standard & Poor's Corporation) examine the historical default rate of the classification of loans, the specific loans in the pool, and the manner in which the loans were selected. These agencies assume the worst general economic conditions in their evaluations.

Credit risk is also affected by both external and internal credit enhancements. External credit enhancements include standby letters of credit, surety bonds, and financial guarantees. When such facilities are used, the credit rating of the asset-backed security is based on that of the party providing the enhancement. Should the credit rating of this party decline, the credit rating of the security will also. Typically, a letter of credit is issued to cover a fixed percentage of the original principal of the underlying loans and is reduced by actual draws. Draws are reimbursed by either the originating lender or a reserve fund. When a commercial bank is the original lender, the reserve fund method is most often used because bank regulators will not permit a bank to treat the transaction as an asset sale unless there is "no recourse" involved in the credit enhancements. A reserve fund satisfies this no-recourse requirement.

A surety bond, or pool insurance, is an insurance contract that protects investors from losses. Most insurers will provide protection only for the entire pool and require that the original structure (without insurance) be eligible for an investment-grade rating. This can be a difficult condition to satisfy. So surety bonds are typically not the primary credit enhancement.

A financial guarantee by the original lender, like a standby letter of credit, usually covers a fixed dollar amount or percentage of the issue. Since the rating of the security depends on the rating of the credit enhancement provider, this form is used primarily by high-rated companies. Also, in the case of commercial banks, the issue of recourse must be addressed in order for the transaction to qualify as a sale of assets.

An asset-backed security also can include an internal credit enhancement. This is accomplished by issuing at least two classes of securities: one senior and one subordinate. The subordinate (junior) class absorbs all default risk while the senior class receives a AA or higher rating. Frequently, the junior class is not rated at all.

All of the features and enhancements associated with asset-backed securities help make them more marketable. Thus, asset-backed securities are an innovation through which U.S. bankers (and other financial institutions) have been able to better manage their lending risk. In the case of those banks that have requested and received permission to operate a Section 20 subsidiary, it is also an area in which they can demonstrate their ability to perform effectively many of the functions of investment banking.

Indexed CDs

Another product innovation of U.S. banks is the indexed certificate of deposit (CD). The Garn-St Germain Act of 1982 gave all depository institutions the power to offer a money market deposit account (MMDA) with an interest rate tied to money market rates. These deposits help banks compete with money market mutual funds. The Market Index Investment Account, offered by Chase Manhattan Bank, is an extension of the MMDA. This deposit has a fixed term with a rate of return that is partially tied to the performance of the S&P500 stock index. Customers select one of three maturities--3 months, 6 months, and 1 year. Within these maturities, an investor can select a specific rate of return formula. For example, for 1-year certificates the choices may be:

- A zero guaranteed minimum return plus 70 percent of the increase in the S&P500 index for the year.
- A 2 percent guaranteed return plus 60 percent of the S&P500 increase for the year.
- A 4 percent guaranteed return plus 40 percent of the S&P500 increase for the year.

An obvious attraction is that the deposit is federally insured for up to $100,000. Moreover, the depositor has a minimum return built in with the possibility of a much higher return. While an investor could conceivably earn a higher rate of return in a stock mutual fund, the mutual fund investment also exposes an investor to the risk of loss of principal. The indexed-CD offers a floor that is not provided in a mutual fund investment.

Other banks now also offer their own version of the Market Index Deposit (MID), with variations that include deposits whose return declines with the stock index or moves with gold prices. These are liabilities whose rate fluctuates with the stock market. On the asset side, issuing banks frequently reduce their portfolio risk by investing in S&P stock index futures contracts. These investments do not violate the Glass-Steagall prohibition against stock investments because contracts are settled in cash rather than in stock.

However, the Internal Revenue Service considers the MID to be two separate instruments: a zero-coupon bond and a call option on a stock index. The option is either exercised at maturity or expires worthless. The issuing institution must stipulate what share of the original purchase price is for the bond and what share represents payment for the option. Each year, the investor pays tax on the imputed bond interest for that period. This information is provided to the investor through a 1099 notice of income earned. If the option component is a nonequity option, gains and losses are deferred until it either expires or is sold. On the other hand, if the option is an equity option, it must be marked to market each year and the appropriate taxes paid.

Because of these complicated tax implications, many banks will sell these instruments only to IRAs or Keogh Accounts.[28] Nevertheless, like the asset-backed security, the indexed CD is an instrument that has enabled commercial banks to cope with the limitations of restrictive regulation.

Swaps

An interest rate swap is the exchange of cash flows between two parties for a specific period of time.[29] The terms of an interest rate swap involve a notional amount, and the interest rate on that notational amount to which each counterparty is obligated. These arrangements help counterparties manage the interest rate risk associated with their asset or liability portfolios. Commercial banks may be either counterparties or intermediaries. An intermediary arranges the transaction, often bringing the two counterparties together. U.S. banks have been instrumental in the development of this market and swaps are a source of fee income to those banks which act as intermediaries.

Banks also can offer swaps to their corporate clients to accommodate their need to manage interest rate risk.

- A floating-rate debt can be transformed into a synthetic fixed-rate debt. The issuer attaches a floating interest rate to the bond. Under the terms of a swap, the issuer agrees to pay a fixed rate and to receive

28. IRAs are Individual Retirement Accounts for employees. Keogh Accounts are retirement accounts for self-employed persons.

29. Foreign currency swaps involve the exchange of currencies at one date and the reversal of the transaction at a specified future date. Currency swaps are derived from parallel loans. In the 1970s, companies in different countries made loans in different currencies to facilitate their multinational operations. In the 1980s, these transactions evolved into currency swaps.

a floating rate on a specified notational principal. The issuer uses the floating rate receipts to satisfy its own interest obligations.

- Likewise, a fixed-rate debt can be converted into a synthetic floating-rate debt. The issuer attaches a fixed interest rate to the bond. In the swap, the issuer agrees to pay a floating rate and receive a fixed rate. Fixed rate receipts satisfy the issuer's obligation.
- An issuer can effectively change the basis used for a floating-rate debt instrument. The bond can be issued with a coupon that floats with LIBOR in the Eurobond market.[30] The swap may be structured to exchange the LIBOR basis for a U.S. Treasury rate basis.
- Interest rate protection can be provided for some specific time period that may be a subset of the full term of a bond. The issuer may be concerned about interest rate exposure for the first two years of a 10-year bond. In this case, a two-year swap contract can provide the needed protection.

These are but a few examples of the uses of swap contracts. Such applications are not limited to bank clients, but may be used by banks themselves to offer competitively structured products and, at the same time, protect against undue interest rate risk.

The concept of swaps has been expanded to other areas. In 1993, the first real estate property swap was constructed. Aldrich Eastman & Waltch, a Boston money management firm, sought to change the asset allocation mix of one of the pension funds that it managed. The objective was to reduce the real estate component in order to invest in the equities market. Selling the real estate in a depressed market would have resulted in a loss, however. Instead the company retained the real estate and agreed to pay the return on the Russell-NCREIF Property Index (a benchmark index that reflects the yield on 1800 properties in the United States). In exchange the fund received the return on a range of U.S. broad-based indexes and several European indexes.

The swap was arranged by Morgan Stanley with a notional amount of $20 million for five years. The firm actually engaged in two transactions: a swap of property-index return for LIBOR, followed by a LIBOR-for-equity swap. The company currently is working on other applications of the concept.

---

30. LIBOR is an acronym for London Interbank Offering Rate.

Within applicable legal constraints, banks can offer equity-related swaps to give themselves and other investors access to foreign markets. These applications are particularly important for banks in their overseas operations and offer a good alternative for tapping into the fast-growing equity markets.

The use of swaps is part of the practice of *financial engineering* in which financial structures are designed that would otherwise not be available. Other tools used in financial engineering are interest rate caps (maximum rate), interest rate floors (minimum rate), options (the right but not the obligation to enter into a future transaction), and swaptions (option on a swap). As major participants in the swap market--as both counterparties and intermediaries--U.S. commercial banks have contributed much in terms of the innovations.

Mezzanine Finance

Mezzanine finance is positioned between senior-level debt and common equity, represents another innovative form of financing in which U.S. commercial banks participate, and is frequently used in "friendly" management buyouts. While there are natural comparisons with the junk bond market, there are some important differences:

- Junk (below investment grade) bond transactions often involve financings of $200 million or more. Mezzanine finance is more often used for transactions of between $3 and $40 million.
- The aggregate junk bond market is well over $100 billion while total mezzanine finance is estimated at $50 billion or less.
- Junk bonds are publicly issued; most mezzanine finance is privately placed or directly negotiated by the issuer with a private purchaser.
- The relatively illiquid nature of mezzanine finance often results in more restrictive covenants than are normally associated with junk bonds, including limits on the issuer's rights to sell assets, incur additional debt, or distribute cash to investors.

U.S. banks have the power to engage in private placements. Thus, mezzanine finance is an area of investment banking that capitalizes on the relationships built up through other banking contacts. The following characteristics are useful in identifying potentially good candidates for mezzazine finance.

- Strong proven operating management at all levels.

- Products that are not subject to rapid technological change.
- Proprietary products with a strong market position.
- Manufacturing efficiencies that qualify the company as a low-cost producer in its industry.
- Products that are sold to industrial customers.
- Cash flow predictability.
- Balance sheet that can support additional leverage.
- Purchase price for the company that does not exceed 8 times operating cash flow.
- Operations not subject to significant import threats.
- Stability of earnings during economic downturns.
- Good asset quality with a substantial share of liquidity assets vis-à-vis fixed assets.
- Quantifiable liabilities.

A typical arrangement will involve the issuance of several classes of securities--both debt and equity. The classifications are *senior debt*, *common equity*, and *mezzanine finance*, which is somewhere in between the first two in terms of risk and reward. The actual proportions of each may be based on the purchase price, for example:

- 60 percent senior debt
- 30 percent mezzanine finance
- 10 percent common equity

These guidelines could also be based on some multiple of operating income, for example:

- senior debt, 4x
- mezzanine finance, 2x
- common equity, .5x

The *senior debt* portion can include a floating interest rate (perhaps, LIBOR plus 2.5 percent), have a term that does not extend beyond than 8 years, and be secured by assets of the firm. Restrictive covenants subordinate the claims of other investors to this class of securities. Purchasers of the senior debt probably would be commercial banks.

Mezzanine finance investors could include high-yield investment companies, private equity companies, and perhaps some senior debt holders. The mezzanine finance instruments can be either senior or junior. Senior mezzanine instruments can pay, for example, 400 to 500 basis points over Treasury and offer some equity participation. The term would be longer than that of senior debt, perhaps 10 to 12 years, with a provision for exit before then.

Junior mezzanine debt would pay a still higher rate, for example, 600 to 800 basis points above Treasury. While the term would be comparable to that of senior mezzanine debt, this instrument would contain fewer restrictive covenants, have warrants or be convertible into common, and may even pay interest in-kind, that is, add scheduled interest to the principal until some specified future date.

Common equity is sold to management, private investors, pension funds, and investment banks. These investors often seek high annual rates of return (40 percent or more) and anticipate an exit in 3 to 7 years.

Mezzanine finance is a vehicle through which medium-sized companies can access capital. U.S. commercial banks fulfill important roles in both structuring and participating in these arrangements.

U.S. Bank Management

The innovation displayed by U.S. banks in product development also reflected in bank management. Under assault from nonbank competitors such as mutual funds, U.S. banks have found the need to reconsider their market positions. In some cases, this has meant expanding their scope of operation. In other cases, it has meant dramatic curtailment of services in specific areas. Citicorp and Bankers Trust present two compelling illustrations.

Citicorp

Citicorp and Citibank, its lead bank, have pursued an agenda of expansion and conquest for several decades. Thus, the purchase of Citicorp by Travelers Group to form the first major U.S. banking and insurance firm in 1998 is not surprising.

During the 1920s, National City Bank followed a strategy to become a financial department store with a strong presence in:

- Retail banking.
- Investment banking, capitalizing on its"placing power," that is, distribution capabilities.
- International finance, including operations in Latin America, the Far East, and Europe.

However, the McFadden and Glass-Steagall Acts seriously altered the bank's expansion plans. Like other money center banks immediately after passage of these legislative measures, Citibank focused on the now more narrowly defined scope of commercial banking activity--accepting deposits and making loans.

It was not until George Moore began to promote his vision for First National City (so renamed after a merger with First National Bank in 1955), that the bank started to distinguish itself. Beginning in the 1950s, Moore, who later became president then chairman, developed the overseas network, expanded the functional scope of the bank's business, upgraded management personnel, and emphasized decentralized decision-making.

The culture of the bank had historically been one in which seniority was the key to advancement. Moore changed this by hiring bright, newly graduated M.B.A.s, and instituting a system of recognition for meritorious performance. His efforts along these lines included personally recruiting students on campus and assuring them that they had a promising and exciting future at First National City Bank. Moore arranged summer internships for students before graduation to stimulate their interest in banking. Once hired, a new crop of management trainees was carefully trained and given full opportunity to compete for promotions.

One of these shining stars was Walter Wriston. Unlike some of his peers, Wriston's academic background did not include business school training. Instead, he had a classical background with a master's degree from the Fletcher School of International Law and Diplomacy. Wriston worked with Moore in the Overseas Division before Moore was named president of the bank in 1959. Wriston shared Moore's vision of the bank as an international presence. The overall plan was to first establish commercial links in other countries, then set up small locations throughout the country, and finally employ the banking expertise shipped in from New York.

Wriston also understood the importance of protecting the bank's deposit base. The large corporate treasurers, who traditionally had invested excess liquidity in large, short-term bank deposits, were being enticed by the issuers of commercial paper. While bank deposits were safer, commercial paper was more liquid because its issuers agreed to buy it back at face value before maturity if an investor required earlier-than-anticipated redemption. Wriston believed a secondary market in bank CDs could neutralize this apparent advantage. In 1960, the "Banker's Certificate" was offered by the Overseas Division and designated as "marketable." The first $1 million certificate was issued to Union Bank of Switzerland, but the initial investor quickly found that there was no market for the certificate.

Wriston then took a more active role in development of a secondary market. He approached Discount Corporation, a government securities dealer, suggesting that the firm make a market in the new certificates. On the condition that First National City provide a $10 million *unsecured* loan to finance the operation (a practice that violated a long-standing rule at the bank), Discount Corporation agreed to do so. In February 1961, the bank announced the new certificates would be sold in $1 million denominations with Discount Corporation making a market in them. Thus, the negotiable CD market was officially launched and would go on to rank second only to the Treasury bill in terms of importance in U.S. money markets.

This head-on approach to banking characterized Wriston's tenure with the bank as he went on to become president in 1967 and CEO in 1970 (retiring in 1984). During his reign, Wriston encouraged the entrepreneurial spirit, established wide-ranging divisions, and championed the cause of deregulation. Wriston was known for pitting his managers against each other, giving an assignment to two different divisions to stimulate in-house competition. As the organization developed into autonomous divisions, this sometimes spilled over to other areas. For instance, product teams sometimes served the same customer without awareness of the others or coordination of their efforts. This type of management created three separate and distinct subcultures within Citicorp: the provision of standardized *consumer* services, the maintenance of long-term relationships with corporate clients in the *institutional bank*, and the expansion of *investment banking* activities.

The *consumer bank* has distinguished the organization in no uncertain terms, with Citicorp being the largest issuer of bank credit cards. The next competitor, Chase Manhattan has only one-fourth of Citicorp's market share. In addition, Citicorp has a formidable presence in the mortgage market, having established an efficient mortgage-processing facility in St. Louis. The consumer/mortgage network has been strengthened by Citicorp's acquisition of troubled savings and loan associations in California, Florida, Illinois, and Washington, D.C. The bank's goal is to develop centralized support mechanisms for a national system of locations that are decentralized enough to deliver customized products.

The *institutional bank* has not shown as much promise. In this division, long-standing corporate customers are served through a combination of products, including foreign exchange, risk management, real estate finance, transaction processing, highly leveraged transactions, asset securitization, and loan syndications. Results have been mixed in this division with notable disappointments in real estate loans to Donald Trump for which the bank was either lead manager or a participant, in senior debt associated with leveraged buyouts, and in real estate loans to Olympia & York in Toronto.

The reverses in commercial banking notwithstanding, Citicorp has faced perhaps even greater challenges in the resumption of *investment banking* activities domestically. Into its new investment bank it also has transferred the treasury functions, mergers & acquisitions, and trading activities. The bank has recruited talented business school graduates and built trading facilities in New York. Other facilities have been established in important financial centers such as London, Tokyo, and Hong Kong. However, there was a certain resistance to paying the high salaries that investment bankers typically command. These strains have, at times, lead to mass resignations of entire groups of investment bankers. While the issue of compensation for commercial vis-à-vis investment bankers is not unique to Citicorp, it seems to have been exacerbated by the strength of the consumer (that is, lower paid) bank within the same organization.

The increase in staff and resources in Citicorp's climate of in-house competition also led to unproductive conflicts during the pursuit of certain deals. For their part, the commercial bankers did not trust the instincts or tactics of the investment bankers. The commercial bankers felt that the investment bankers had little loyalty for the bank and were interested only in their own transactions and bonuses.

The bankers on the investment side tend to be more entrepreneurial and unorthodox, while those on the commercial side are more sensitive to organizational goals and protocol. As a result, giving investment bankers managerial responsibilities often did not work well.

As a remedy for these problems, Citicorp consolidated the investment and institutional banks in 1987. There is a division of labor in the new unit: institutional bankers originate deals and investment bankers execute them and perform trading functions.

Bankers Trust

Bankers Trust was founded as a trust company in 1903 to provide New York money center banks with a reputable trust operation to which they could refer their commercial and investment banking clients. It fulfilled this function until the 1913 Federal Reserve Act also gave commercial banks the right to engage in trust activities. From that point on, Bankers Trust developed as a full-service commercial bank with securities underwriting capabilities and international operations. During this developmental phase, Bankers Trust became known primarily as a wholesale bank.

Its involvement in retail banking began primarily after World War II when pent-up consumer demand was unleashed. Financing for homes, automobiles, and appliances was a growth industry for banks and other financial institutions. Bankers Trust opened branch offices throughout the state of New York.

At the same time, the institution expanded its overseas facilities with representation in 30 countries and correspondent relationships with 1200 banks. In addition, specialized groups were developed in areas such as oil and gas, construction, and public utilities. The bank was one of the first to computerize its support functions.

Profits were healthy during the 1950s and 1960s, but began to deteriorate in the 1970s. The bank analyzed its management approach and took the dramatic step in 1971 of significantly reducing its workforce. This was rare in the banking industry, where lifetime employment had been virtually assured. In further restructuring the following year, Bankers Trust discontinued its stock transfer and related activities.

Then, as the bank continued to review its position in various markets, the real estate market in New York City suffered major reverses in the mid-1970s. Bankers Trust had made loans to real estate developers and to real estate investment trusts (REITs) that supported construction and real estate development. A subsidiary of the bank even advised a REIT named Bankers Trust Mortgage Investors. With an exposure of almost $700 million, Bankers Trust suffered major losses.

At the same time, challenges to the retail area arose. Citibank announced that it would invest $100 million in automated teller machines (ATMs). By the time of this announcement, Bankers Trust had expanded its branch network, but not to the same extent as other money center banks. Retail banking contributed only 10 percent of total revenues. Under the circumstances, competing with Citicorp's investment in ATMs did not appear feasible. In 1978, the difficult decision to exit retail banking was made in 1978. Both the retail branches and the credit card operation had been sold by 1982.

Beginning in 1978, Bankers Trust became a *wholesale* institution with major divisions in:

- Wholesale banking (traditional corporate loans)
- Fiduciary operations (trust and private banking)
- Capital markets (government and municipal bond underwriting and trading)
- Corporate finance (mergers and acquisitions)

Although substantial investments were made in the capital markets and corporate finance divisions, Bankers Trust continued to emphasize the wholesale business. This focus remained its strength up to the point that Bankers Trust was acquired by Deutsche Bank in 1999. In fact, Deutsche Bank's focus on global investment banking was no doubt a strong incentive for this purchase.

Over time, however, the investment banking culture began to emerge. First, the corporate finance group was organized into five areas--mergers and acquisitions, public finance, private placements, leveraged buyout equity financing, and leasing. Members of this group worked apart from the commercial bankers and received performance-related bonuses--bonuses that tended to alienate the commercial bankers, as was the case at Citicorp. In addition, under the leadership of Charles Sanford (who would become president in 1983 and CEO in 1987), the capital markets group positioned itself more like a Wall Street firm than commercial bank. It was physically established in separate facilities in the Wall Street area and paid competitive salaries and bonuses. In the late 1970s and early 1980s, Sanford's power within the bank increased and he persistently argued for more emphasis on investment banking.

Beginning in 1983, Bankers Trust redefined its mission as that of a full-service investment bank. Accountability in the bank has shifted from a common pool of resources that is spread throughout the bank to individual profit centers. The exact configuration is always subject to change based on market conditions, but the major areas of operation are:

- Financial services (merchant and investment banking)
- Global markets (corporate finance)
- Nonbanking activities (investment management and other activities)

Bankers Trust has emerged as an interesting contrast to Citicorp. While Citicorp also has a decentralized organizational structure, there appears to be more coordination between divisions at Bankers Trust. Having eliminated its retail functions, Bankers Trust is a smaller, more agile organization. Because of its trading and investment banking focus, Bankers Trust also has a more volatile earnings stream than Citicorp. Citicorp has made a substantial investment, perhaps more than any other U.S. bank, in consumer banking. Bankers Trust elected to exit the retail market altogether.

Universal Banking in Germany

In contrast to the United States, Germany banking is more stable and predictable. This is primarily because the German economy is bank-centered. In their pivotal role, German banks routinely engage in *universal banking* that is, the provision of all financial services. The strong bonds that tie German businesses to German banks present a fascinating case study in client relations.

Client Relations

Almost from the beginning, German banks have been major shareholders in German companies and have had representation on boards of directors. This presence is observable in both large and small firms.

Large firms in Germany often developed in regions which there was not even a local handicraft infrastructure. This meant that a firm was forced to build capacity for all necessary components within the firm itself, requiring massive capital infusions. German banks provided these funds. The first products were large machinery such as locomotives and steel-making equipment. Later, the firms diversified into other areas of machinery to maintain employment and operational stability.

Because the European market was composed of dissimilar product standards and preferences, large German companies often manufactured high-quality products in short production runs. Employees were skilled at every phase of their jobs so as to accommodate these rapid changes. In this sense, the large companies became adept at reacting to changing market conditions. If shareholders had not understood these dynamics, dedicated capital would have been much more difficult to secure. As major shareholders, German banks were less concerned with temporary fluctuations and more concerned with long-term viability of their clients.

Deutsche Bank is the largest of the three major universal banks in Germany. (The other two are Dresdner Bank and Commerzbank.) It is also one of Germany's largest shareholders. Its equity stakes include:

- Daimler-Benz (automotives)
- Allianz (Europe's largest insurance company)
- Munich Re (world's largest re-insurance company)
- Karstadt (trading company)
- Philip Holzmann (construction)
- Heidelberger Zement (construction materials)
- Hapag Lloyd (shipping)
- Metallgesellschaft (industrial group)

Moreover, Deutsche Bank managers occupy more than 400 seats on the boards of other German firms.

While the three large universal banks have established relationships with major firms, other German banks have fueled growth within the *Mittelstand* group--a group of small- and medium-sized firms. The larger industrial firms developed in regions without a handicraft or supplier infrastructure, but the Mittelstand firms emerged in regions with considerable infrastructure. In these areas, there was little need for each firm to construct facilities to provide all components of production. Firms remained relatively small and usually family-owned. Financing often came in the form of cooperative banks, similar in form and function to credit unions.

Over time, even smaller firms became involved in the export drive of the German economy and more advanced banking services were required. As incomes grew in the late 1950s and 1960s, overall liquidity increased. Savings banks, regional banks, and credit cooperatives offered a full range of loans and other financial services to Mittelstand companies.

There is also a trend toward "network" financing. Traditionally, the House Bank or main bank provides the full range of services for a particular client. In a network arrangement, several banks provide financing for a network of commercial or industrial firms. Network bank representatives sit on the boards of network industrial firms and vice versa. This is quite similar to the Japanese *keiretsu* arrangement in the sense that there are interlocking relationships between groups of financial and industrial firms. Thus, in both large and small firms, there are close ties between banking and commercial firms.

An interesting byproduct of this system is that the takeover phenomenon of the 1980s in the United States was not witnessed in Germany. Continuity of management in Germany is continued quite important. German banks, as major shareholders generally adopt the view that industrial management must not be constrained in making appropriate long-term decisions by the prospect of a hostile takeover.

This is in sharp contrast to the situation in the United States, where other institutional investors, including pensions funds, mutual funds, and insurance companies, hold 50 percent of publicly traded stock. The difference in the United States is that institutional investors are evaluated in terms of the rate of return they generate in the short-term. Since this rate of return is measured solely in terms of dividend yield and capital gains yield, investments that payoff in the long-term often have negative short-term consequences with respect to earnings (and hence dividends and stock prices). Industrial managers are increasingly coming under fire by these so-called "supershareholders." While the concerns of institutional investors may indeed be warranted in many cases, there is no doubt that U.S. industry has adopted a much more short-term focus than its German counterpart.

In fact, German industrial firms and banks have been known to work together to prevent an unwanted foreign takeover. For example, in 1990 Deutsche Bank worked to block the acquisition of Continental AG, a German tire maker, by Pirelli SpA, the well-known Italian firm. When Leopoldo Pirelli (head of the Italian firm) first approached Ulrich Weiss (the Deutsche Bank representative who sat as head of Continental's board), Weiss was generally receptive to the idea of a merger. The combination would help enhance the presence of Deutsche Bank in the larger European arena and boost the value of the bank's 5 percent stake in Continental. Furthermore, if the two companies combined, the new firm would control 15 percent of the world tire market, only slightly below the 17 percent share held by Bridgestone.

Nevertheless, Horst Urban of Continental believed that the Pirelli overtures were a thinly veiled hostile takeover. After all, Pirelli had begun to buy Continental shares even before the talks began. Furthermore, the terms of the DM2 billion deal were unacceptable. Under Pirelli's plan, Continental would buy Pirelli shares at a premium over their market value. Continental was to raise the cash for this deal by both issuing more stock and borrowing funds. The projected operational savings of DM400 million per year appeared exaggerated in Urban's view. Besides which, Pirelli had not revealed who was actually buying Continental shares. If there were unknown investors involved on Pirelli's side, this would tend to establish the hostility of the offer. This seemed especially true in light of the commonly adopted corporate rule that no single shareholder can exercise more than 5 percent of voting rights, regardless of shareholdings. Multiple parties on Pirelli's side could sidestep this provision and force the merger.

After reviewing Urban's objections, a somewhat embarrassed Weiss reversed his earlier endorsement of the merger and the rest of the Continental board members followed suit. Then Urban enlisted the support of Continental's clients, including Daimler-Benz, BMW, and Volkswagen. Even Allianz, the insurance giant that is partially owned by Deutsche Bank, joined in the defensive front. Together, these German companies formed a pool to buy a 25 percent shareholder interest in Continental. This was enough to block the merger because German corporate law stipulates that no major decision affecting a company may be made with less than 75 percent of the voting shareholders. In addition to this 25-percent block, Deutsche Bank controlled (via proxy) shares that it held in trust.

In response to this obvious show of power, Pirelli attempted to negotiate somewhat more reasonable terms, but Urban refused to discuss the matter. Meanwhile, Continental suffered business reverses that led to the closing of some of its General Tire production facilities in the United States. At this point, Deutsche Bank (again) reversed its position and supported the merger. When Weiss met with Pirelli to discuss the possibility of reopening negotiations, Pirelli agreed on the condition that Urban not act as the negotiator for Continental. Not long thereafter, Horst Urban was replaced by Hubertus Von Grünberg, a previous employee of ITT in the United States.

The talks were aborted, however, when it was revealed that the financial situation of Pirelli was worse than Continental had realized. Urban's earlier suspicions were confirmed, albeit belatedly. Other investors were involved on Pirelli's side and, in fact, Pirelli had guaranteed to cover any losses they sustained. The losses turned out to be substantial--approximately $300 million.

The failed Continental takeover helps illustrate the power of German banks and the close relationships between banks and industrial firms. This environment contributes to a more stable environment in which industrial managers are not as subject to the threat of hostile takeovers as is true in the United States. Also, the short-term-profits pressure is not as intense because pension funds are primarily managed within the companies that sponsor the plans and large mutual funds are managed by banks. Thus far, German insurance companies have shown no desire to assert their shareholder rights in any way that seriously challenges traditional German methods of cooperation.

German Bank Management

The Deutsche Bank also provides some insight into the management of German banks. Before his death in a terrorist bombing in 1989, Alfred Herrhausen pursued an agenda of making Deutsche Bank a truly global presence. In contrast, his successor, Hilmar Kopper, is inclined to adopt a somewhat less expansionist position.

Herrhausen was a trained economist and an experienced industrialist when he joined Deutsche Bank at the end of the 1960s. At that time, the bank barely ventured beyond national borders. Post-war trauma in German banking had included the break-up of the "Big Three." Even after this initial division was reversed, the mood remained tentative. Having reached maturity after the war, Herrhausen did not share these reservations.

He joined the bank's board in 1970 and set the course. He felt the need to build for the future--not just the Single European Market of 1992, but the global economy of the 21st century. Under Herrhausen's leadership, the bank began to take risks in a more entrepreneurial spirit. His was an independent spirit that would not even entertain the notion of a joint venture. Instead, the bank made wide-ranging international acquisitions.

Location	Acquired Firm
London (England)	Morgan Grenfell (merchant bank)
Amsterdam (Netherlands)	H. Albert de Bary (stockbroker)
Vienna (Austria)	Antoni Hacker (private bank)
Milan (Italy)	Banca d'America e d'Italia (commercial bank)
Barcelona (Spain)	Banco Commercial Transatlantico (commercial bank)
Toronto (Canada)	McLean McCarthy (stockbroker)

Buenos Aires (Argentina)	Bank of America branches (commercial bank)
Sydney (Australia)	Bain & Co. (stockbroker)

Hilmar Kopper assumed leadership after Herrhausen's death. Unlike his predecessor, Kopper has had a lifelong career in banking. In fact, he entered Deutsche Bank as a trainee immediately after completing his education. His strength is considered to be his technical banking background rather than his strategic vision. He believes that the key to success is a healthy home market, in which he includes the Single European Market.

In its 1994 annual report, Deutsche Bank reveals its new strategy, the "Closer to the Customer" project. The bank intends to improve its service offerings to customers in terms of quality, speed, and price of banking services. The decision-making process has been shortened and staff at the local branch level has been given more responsibility in order to encourage greater entrepreneurial behavior. Deutsche Bank has embarked on a quality improvement program that includes constant dialogue with customers.

The impact of the securities industry in world economics and the German capital markets is also reflected in the composition of Germany's retail client base. Deutsche Bank now has one million self-employed individuals or small businesses among its retail banking clients. The division has been renamed Retail Banking and Trade Customers. Interestingly, 60% of customer deposits and investments are related to securities portfolios, with only 40% representing deposits.

Deutsche Bank has placed strong emphasis on the development of its investment banking operations. Late in 1994, the bank announced its decision to merge its Frankfurt-based investment banking operations with those of its London subsidiary, Morgan Grenfell. Deutsche Bank customers expect that their investment bankers will be able to provide them with a wide range of services in both domestic and international markets. The domestic customers continue to be serviced by the Frankfurt office.

Historically, German companies and investors have been much more interested in bond markets than in equity markets because of their unusual sensitivity to the threat of inflation. Increasingly, however, the large

German companies are becoming more interested in issuing equity as a source of funding.

London was selected for the consolidated operation because of its historic role as a trading center. It is believed that London also has the talent and diversity of skills that enable Deutsche Bank's investment banking operation to evolve into truly world-class status.

Deutsche Bank will continue to wield considerable power in German industry, as will Dresdner Bank and Commerzbank. One of the primary challenges for the German banking system will be to compete more effectively in international capital markets. In this bank-dominated economy, certain phases of financial services have not been as well developed as they might otherwise have been. For example, stock of medium-sized firms is often not widely traded. Also, when issues are brought to the public market, there are indications that there may not always be as much free competition as should exist. Even a major industry firm may alternate the underwriting of its common stock issues between two of the major banks. If, for a particular reason, that firm wishes not to award the underwriting to the bank whose turn it is next, its wishes to engage the other bank may be refused precisely because it is not that bank's turn.

Without a doubt, the strong central and dedicated capital of German banks has been one of the critical factors in the development of the German economy. A less desirable side effect of this arrangement, however, has been less innovative banking and capital market developments. As the Single European Market continues to evolve, German banks may find it necessary to look for alliances with institutions that have made greater strides in terms of refining new financial services.

International Traditional in the United Kingdom

While Germany has remained relatively insulated from the impact of aggressive competition, the British banking system has become one of the most internationalized in the world. With this openness to foreign influences, it has been touched by some of the same innovation noted in the United States and has been forced to manage change associated with the "Big Bang" and the Single European Market.

A Diverse Financial Market

The financial system of the United Kingdom shares attributes with both its German and U.S. counterparts. Its banking system is dominated by a few large institutions--Barclays, National Westminster, Midland, and Lloyds--as is the case in German. At the same time, a vibrant community of other financial services firms exists, as in the United States. This perhaps paradoxical situation is the result of a highly concentrated financial district referred to as the City that has developed a particular expertise in international trade and investment. The City both operates and "thinks" on a global scale.

The factors contributing to this focus are a tradition of international finance, ties from past colonial relationships, and the Euromarket development. London is one of the three most important cities in foreign exchange markets along with New York and Tokyo. During the 1980s, the volume of foreign exchange trading in London was often twice as great as that in the other two cities combined. Before the U.S. dollar became the most dominant world currency, the British pound held this distinction.

In terms of the international connections of British clearing banks, Barclays and Lloyds have long-standing operations in Africa and Latin America, respectively. Midland and National Westminster have expanded into international markets primarily by building in-house expertise and through overseas acquisitions. Standard Chartered is the result of a merger between Standard Bank (with sizeable interests in Africa) and Chartered Bank (with significant interests in the Far East). Hong Kong and Shanghai Banking Corporation (HSBC) is not a typical British bank. Until recently, the head office of HSBC was in Hong Kong. With its acquisition of Midland Bank in the United Kingdom, HSBC moved its headquarters to London. Thus, British banks, over time, have been completely at ease in international transactions and have freely invested overseas.

With respect to the attractions of the City for foreign banks, one of them is that London is situated in the middle time zone that links New York and Tokyo. It is possible to talk to Tokyo in the early morning and New York in the afternoon. Another critical factor has been that London did not have laws that separated commercial and investment banking or that restricted the rates of interest on deposits. Eurodollar deposits were issued in London without the constraint of interest rate ceilings. Eurobonds in first dollars, then yen and deutsche marks, were issued in London.

Ironically, British banks did not participate in early Eurobond issuances as much as other institutions. One reason for this is that the United Kingdom imposed currency exchange controls on nonresident sterling transactions until 1979. The British banks were thus not familiar with the new instruments initially and exhibited a certain amount of hesitancy to become involved.

Where the British firms feared to tread, foreign firms rushed in. When exchange controls were lifted British fund managers began to invest overseas vigorously. After two years, it was found that 95 percent of these overseas investments were being handled by nonBritish firms. It was this foreign presence in the bond and stock markets that convinced the Bank of England and the U.K. government to orchestrate the Big Bang in 1986. Under this initiative, British securities firms became more competitive and banks were encouraged to invest in securities activities. It is clear that the international nature of the British financial markets is firmly established.

British Bank Management

Barclays Bank is one of the largest British institutions. Unlike HSBC Holdings, Barclays Bank is a distinctly British bank with long ties to the United Kingdom and Europe. The institution has also undergone significant restructuring to meet the challenges of the banking in a more competitive environment.

Barclays was founded in London in 1736 when James Barclay joined a family goldsmithing and banking firm under the loco of a black spread eagle. As other family members joined the firm, it became known as Barclays, Bevan & Tritton (1782). When banking law changed in Britain in the late 19th century, 20 firms merged to avoid takeover and became Barclay & Co (1896). Over the next 20 years, Barclay & Co. acquired another 20 institutions. In 1917, the name was changed to Barclays Bank.

Barclays was well positioned to participate in the economic expansion that followed World War II. By the 1950s, it had surpassed Midland Bank to become the largest of the British clearing banks. Its nationwide branch network was linked by computer in 1959 and it introduced the BarclayCard (credit card) in conjunction with BankAmerica in 1966. Barclays also expanded internationally. It acquisitions and subsidiaries in the United States include:

- Acquisition of American Credit, consumer finance (1980).

- Subsidiary BarclaysAmerican, with 138 finance offices purchased from Beneficial (1980).
- New York subsidiary, with 31 branches purchased from Bankers Trust (1982).

After the 1983 announcement of the Big Bang, Barclays restructured itself as a holding company. Its major thrust into the securities industry was the formation of Barclays de Zoete Wedd, a merger of its own merchant bank with broker de Zoete Bevan and jobber Wedd Durlacher. The combination has been successful by any measure. In a recent survey of merchant brokers, Barclays de Zoete Wedd was ranked among the top 10 firms in the industry--seventh in quality of service, sixth in quality of management and community responsibility, fifth in value as a long-term investment, fourth in ability to attract and retain top talent and capacity to innovate, third in quality of marketing, and first in financial soundness. In addition, in 1993 the firm ranked high in terms of its activities as lead manager in the Euromarkets:

- Third in Euro-Australian bonds (A$450 million)
- Second in Eurosterling bonds (£3.5 billion)

This is not to suggest that Barclays has been unaffected by difficult economic conditions. Barclays sustained its first-ever operating loss in 1992, amounting to $366 million. This loss was a result of ill-conceived investments geared primarily to maintain its stature as the British bank with the largest asset base (that is, before HSBC acquired Midland). The bulk of the proceeds from an earlier $1.4 billion rights offering was invested in real estate in Britain and North America. An estimated total write-off of $400 million was necessary in connection with Olympia & York. A poor consumer market in the United States also hurt profits.

Barclays Bank has been forced to sell its California banking operation to Wells Fargo (1988), its consumer finance operation in the United States to Primerica's Commercial Credit (1989), and its consumer banking operation to Bank of New York (1992).

In 1991, Barclays restructured itself into four main division:

- Commercial Banking
- Finance
- Service Businesses
- Barclays de Zoete Wedd (BZW)

The bank initiated a cost-cutting program that included eliminating 5,000 jobs in 1991, 2,300 in 1992, and an additional 15,000 by 1997.

Analysts blame the management at Barclays for these problems. The leadership of the bank consistently has been drawn from the families associated with the original 20 banks that formed Barclay & Co. in 1896. In almost 100 years, all but two chairman were selected from the descendants of these families. Critics charge that the close family links have blocked the adoption of strong management techniques with respect to investments and operations.

In 1992, the position of Chairman was separated from that of Chief Executive. In 1993, the position of Chief Executive was filled by Martin Taylor, formerly Chairman and Chief Executive of the manufacturer Courtaulds Textiles. This appointment brings Barclays into a new era of management. Taylor had never worked in a bank but used his managerial and communications skills (he also speaks Mandarin) to institute change that produced better returns on capital. His perspectives provide interesting insights into the new banking environment in the United Kingdom and Europe. For example, he believes that:

- Banks were slow to recognize how dangerous their basic banking business had become during the 1980s.
- The disintermediation of corporate debt has fundamentally changed the business of Barclays Bank.
- U.K. banks are quickly becoming leaders in all domestic financial service markets, not just banking.
- Barclays is well positioned to take a major share of the fund management and life insurance businesses.

In order to capture these opportunities, Barclays made significant changes in its corporate culture to move from a retail bank to an asset management firm.

In June 1995, Barclays made major strides in its goal to incorporate money management in its business portfolio. After three months of negotiation, the bank agreed to buy Wells Fargo Nikko Investment Advisors for $440 million. This was the first major acquisition by Barclays since Martin Taylor became CEO in 1993. San Francisco-based Wells Fargo Nikko was jointly owned by Wells Fargo & Co. and Nikko Securities Co. and is the world's largest money manager using quantitative-investment techniques, overseeing $180 billion in client funds.[31] Including the assets under management at BZW Asset Management, Barclays manages more

[31] Quantitative managers follow highly disciplined investment strategies, including operating index funds that attempt to match the performance of selected market indexes.

than $250 billion, making it one of the world's largest asset managers in any industry. The only two firms with more assets under management are Japan's Nippon Life (more than $375 billion) and Fidelity Investments (more than $325 billion).

In this deal, Barclays has also bought the MasterWorks division of Wells Fargo, which provides investment and administrative support for defined-contribution pension funds. The new company targets Europe, bringing quantitative technology to the United Kingdom. This acquisition helps Barclays to address the challenge in Europe of improved private pension systems. It is also entirely possible that such expertise can be transferred to Asia--a region of modest development of private pension funds--where Barclays already has 2,000 employees.

Barclays is being no less aggressive in the retail banking market. To contain costs it has reduced the number of branches from 2,800 to 2,000. At the same time, the bank is emphasizing cross selling of products in those branches that remain. Traditional banking products are offered as well as mortgages and travel insurance. Although the credit card business in Europe has become increasingly competitive, the Barclay card continues to attract customers. Features of the Barclay card continue to maintain strong client interest such as a help line that offers free legal service and associated car repair service.

The trends of product development and resource allocation in Barclays are indications of the future of banking in Europe. The traditional lending and deposit activities will be supplemented by more asset management and fee-generating business.

The Quest for International Competitiveness in Japan

There are clear contradictions in the role of Japan in international banking. On one hand, Japanese banks top the list of the world's largest. On the other hand, their entry into international banking has been characterized by a series of progressive steps in terms of their range of financial activities. These contradictions are best explained in the context of the Japanese philosophies of international conquest and domestic cooperation.

Measured Steps Toward Internationalization

The philosophy of international conquest by Japanese banks is framed by the objective of supporting the companies within their respective *keiretsu* groups. In the 1960s and 1970s, Japanese banks took extraordinary steps to understand the industries that they served, sending hundreds of executives to the companies for assignments in financial, marketing, technical or planning departments. Within a bank, departments were set up to:

- Track macroeconomic trends.
- Study specific industry segments.
- Perform detailed industrial market surveys.
- Retain engineers that evaluated both foreign patents and the technological competence of the bank's clients.

Thus, the driving motivation was not so much to advance the bank as to advance the fortunes of bank clients.

When bank customers moved overseas, Japanese banks followed. The Euromarkets were attractive to both Japanese industrial and banking firms. However, the unrestricted market was a challenge to the delicate balance between banks and securities firms. The negotiations surrounding the Euromarket participation of Japanese banks served to temper their quest for market share.

By the time Euromarkets developed, lines of demarcation had been drawn between banks and securities firms in the bond markets. In the 1920s, however, banks were free to underwrite corporate bonds, hold them in their own portfolios, or sell them to securities firms for distribution to the public. Japanese exports to Europe were healthy in light of the consumer and industrial needs of that war-torn region. When the European economy recovered, Japanese exports collapsed. Many bond issuers defaulted, bondholders lost their entire investment, and the Ministry of Finance was forced to support a number of banks. Even with this support, the number of banks shrank from 1283 in 1927 to 538 in 1932.

In the midst of the financial confusion, the Ministry of Finance drafted legislation in 1927 that gave the Ministry broad regulatory oversight in exchange for its protection and the assurance that there would be no further entries into the banking industry. Next, the largest 30 bond-underwriting banks formed the Bond Issue Arrangement Committee. With the approval of the Ministry of Finance, the Bond Committee established rules such that no future bonds were to be issued without sufficient collateral. Furthermore, only "trustee banks" would hold the bond collateral, earning a fee for their services. Eight banks, including the Industrial Bank of Japan formed the core of the Bond Committee. Securities firms were allowed as underwriting members. But only banks could earn the collateral fee. Moreover, the Ministry of Finance blocked attempts by securities firms to acquire trustee banks.

The whole arrangement was effectively designed to reduce corporate reliance on bond financing and increase reliance on bank financing. Even after the imposition of Article 65 by Occupation Forces following World War II, the Bond Committee remained intact. Article 65 permitted banks to underwrite only private placement bonds, thus establishing similar rules to those in the United States, but did not disband the Bond Committee.

Allied Forces had banned all financial institutions from issuing bonds on the premise that bank bonds would compete excessively with industrial bonds, limiting capital available to commercial firms. This ban was lifted in 1950 and, one year later, the Bank of Tokyo was permitted to issue bonds with 3-year maturities. Three long-term credit banks and eight trust banks were given similar privileges but with 7-year maturities. The Bank of Tokyo specialized in international finance, had few domestic offices, and represented little threat in the domestic market. The long-term bonds of the long-term credit and trust banks would not compete with short-term deposits. All other banks were precluded from bond issuance.

In the 1970s, the oil-price shock induced recessionary conditions in Japan which, in turn, led industrial corporations to seek cheaper sources of funds. The Euromarkets offered such alternatives. The Ministry of Finance stipulated asset and capital requirements for any firm issuing Eurobonds. Nevertheless, the instruments were an attractive form of financing for those firms that qualified because there were no collateral requirements, no mandatory prospectuses, and lower interest rates. Moreover, the firms had access to variable rate instruments and swaps that were not available domestically. In the first half of the 1970s, the Euromarket accounted for 1.7 percent of Japanese corporate fund raising. In the second half of the decade, the percent was 19.6 percent.

Japanese commercial banks followed their clients and established wholly-owned investment bank subsidiaries or formed joint ventures with British banks. After all, there were no Article 65 restrictions in the Euromarket.

This activity did not go unchallenged, however. In 1969 when a subsidiary of the Bank of Tokyo participated in an underwriting for Honda

Motors that was led by Goldman Sachs and Nikko Securities, the securities industry reacted to this offshore encroachment on their territory.[32] Such activity could easily lead to obvious violations of Article 65. What would prevent the banks from negotiating all terms on Japanese soil and simply booking the transaction in London? The Ministry of Finance reacted with a characteristically Japanese compromise. The banks were not forbidden to underwrite in the Euromarket. Instead, they were told that they should not actively solicit business clients from Japan. All other potential clients were allowed in an unrestricted manner.

When Fuji-Kleinwort Benson, a Fuji Bank joint venture, acted as a managing underwriter for a Eurobond issue by Canon in 1974, the Securities industry reacted once again. This was even worse than the Bank of Tokyo participation. It was a lead management role by a bank with a large branch network--a network that could be used to pursue other Japanese firms as potential underwriting clients. Together, three bureaus of the Ministry of Finance (Banking, Securities, and International Finance) issued a statement warning foreign subsidiaries not to violate the spirit of Article 65 and reminding banks in foreign joint ventures to be sensitive to their own portfolio positions and not hold too much of a specific issue in their own asset portfolios.

This pronouncement was not much in the way of a prohibition. Later the same year, the Industrial Bank of Japan applied to the International Finance Bureau for a license to open a wholly-owned subsidiary for the purpose of securities transactions in the Euromarket. This led to what was referred to as the Three Bureaus Agreement in which the Banking, Securities, and International Finance Bureaus stipulated that:

- Banks and securities firms should cooperate in the Euromarkets.
- Banks should not use their domestic branch networks to solicit clients for their European securities operations.
- Banks should not negotiate with their Euromarket clients within Japanese national boundaries.
- Banks should not act against the spirit of Article 65.
- Banks should be mindful of the order of the institutions listed on issuance announcements.

Banks could operate in the Euromarkets as long as they did not take a more prominent position than the securities firms. The development of this

[32] Bank of Tokyo later merged with Mitsubishi Bank to become Bank of Tokyo-Mitsubishi.

compromise illustrates the measured steps toward internationalization that Japanese banks have taken. It also helps to explain why they have used such aggressive pricing tactics in the pursuit of loan business. At least this was an area in which their right to operate would not be challenged.

Japanese Bank Management

In their international expansion, Japanese banks have felt less able to compete with their counterparts from other countries because of regulatory constraints. They at least partially compensated for this by purchasing foreign expertise. A partial list of such acquisitions in the United States includes:

Japanese Bank	Target Firm
Sumitomo	Goldman Sachs (investment bank, $500 million)
Fuji	Walter E. Heller (finance company, $425 million)
Sanwa	Leasing affiliate of Continental ($500 million)
Mitsui[33]	Finance affiliate of Security Pacific ($100 million)
Dai-Ichi Kangyo	CIT Financial ($1.4 billion)

All the while, Japanese banks continued an aggressive program of lending both at home and abroad. Like banks in other countries, overextension in declining real estate markets has hurt profits. The manner in which these losses have been handled in Japan, however, is unusual. Presumably in an attempt to maintain stability in the banking markets, nonperforming loans were not reported until they had failed to pay principal and/or interest for one year. Banks were even more reluctant to actually write-off the loans because there was no tax benefit to doing so. Write-offs are not deductible if the loan is collateralized and the borrower is not yet bankrupt.

---

33. Mitsui is now part of Sakura Bank, the product of a merger between Mitsui and Taiyo Kobe.

Banks offer fees to firms like trading companies to purchase real estate with the understanding that they will buy it back at an agreed upon premium in perhaps five years. Led by the officials in the Ministry of Finance, Japanese banks and industrial firms attempt to share the pain of any necessary restructuring. This process is an indication of the power of the *keiretsu* system in Japanese. Just as the banks positioned themselves to be supportive of industrial firms in the 1960s and 1970s, it should not be surprising that the industrial firms be called upon to assist the banks in some measure under current circumstances.

Conclusion

German and Japanese banks have perhaps the best relations with their commercial clients among the industrialized countries of the world. However, both systems face specific challenges. While legally free to do so, German banks have not tended to develop innovations that could be considered on the cutting edge of financial technology. Japanese banks on the other band, face regulatory constraints that inhibit their scope of services. Banks in the United States and the United Kingdom have not developed the same kind of client relations as their counterparts in Germany and Japan but have developed markets and products that have led the way to financial innovation. The possibility of global strategic alliances suggests that these individual strengths can lead to the formation of powerful institutions that can better serve both consumer and industrial markets in the 21st century.

Selected References

Bennett, Rosemary. "Rocket Scientists Produce a Fresh Wave of Solutions," *Euromoney,* March 1993, pp. 46-54.

"Branching Out: Japanese in Asia," *The Economist*, August 7, 1993, p. 69.

de Carmoy, Herve. *Global Banking Strategy: Financial Markets and Industrial Decay,* Basil Blackwell, Cambridge, Massachusetts, 1990.

Chai, Alan, Alta Campbell, and Patrick J. Spain. *Hoover's Handbook of World Business*, The Reference Press, Austin, Texas, 1993.

Chew, Donald, Editor. *New Developments in Commercial Banking*, Blackwell Finance, Cambridge, Massachusetts, 1991.

Coulbeck, Neil. *The Multinational Banking Industry*, New York University Press, New York, 1984.

"The Deutsche Bank Juggernaut Will Keep on Rolling," *Euromoney*, January 1990, pp. 33-44.

Dwyer, Paula and Kelley Holland. "At Barclays, A Stiff Upper Lip No Longer Suffices," *Business Week*, April 12, 1993, p. 80.

Feldman, Amy. "CDs for CPAs," *Forbes*, July 19, 1993, pp. 92-95.

Glouchevitch, Philip. *Juggernaut; The German Way of Business: Why It Is Transforming Europe--and the World*, Simon & Schuster, New York, 1992.

"Hidden Jewels: Bank Branches," *The Economist*, January 9, 1993, pp. 71-72.

Hilton, Anthony. *City Within A State*, I.B. Tauris, London, 1987.

Katzenstein, Peter J. *Industry and Politics in West Germany: Toward the Third Republic*, Cornell University Press, Ithaca, New York, 1989.

Kearns, Robert L. *Zaibatsu America: How Japanese Firms Are Colonizing Vital U.S. Industries*, The Free Press, New York, 1992.

Kim, James. "Steffen Takes His Scissors to Citicorp," *USA Today*, May 21, 1993, p. 3B.

Lee, Peter. "Capitalizing on Distressed Real Estate," *Euromoney*, March 1993, pp. 58-62.

"A Loan Sale to the Rescue? (Japanese Banks)," *The Economist*, November 30, 1991, pp. 78-79.

Middleton, Sir Peter. "Rapid Change and The Opportunities It Presents Investment Banking," *The Economist*, May 2, 1992, pp. 1-5.

Miller, Richard B. *Citicorp: The Story of a Bank In Crisis*, McGraw-Hill, New York, 1993.

Muolo, Paul. "Are Reverses Set to Advance?" United States Banker, May 1993, pp. 28-30.

"New Dreams at Deutsche Bank," *The Economist*, June 22, 1991, pp. 79-82.

"The New Look: Barclay's Bank, *The Economist*, December 12, 1992, p. 86.

"On the Mend: British Bank," *The Economist*, August 7, 1993, pp. 67-68.

"Overburdened: Japanese Banks," *The Economist*, July 25, 1992, pp. 77-78.

Robinson, Danielle. "Tailored For All Tastes," *Euromoney*, February 1993, pp. 63-64.

Rodgers, David. *The Future of American Banking: Managing for Change*, McGraw-Hill, New York, 1993.

Rosenbluth, Frances McCall. *Financial Politics in Contemporary Japan*, Cornell University Press, Ithaca, New York, 1989.

Simon, Hermann. "Lessons from Germany's Midsize Giants," *Harvard Business Review,* March-April 1992, pp. 115-123.

Smith, Eric Owen. "Equity Stakes: Are U.K. Banks Following the German Pattern?" *Banking World*, June 1991, pp. 28-30.

6. Forging Financial Services Alliances

Introduction

Deregulation, European market integration, privatization of state-owned enterprises, and the emergence of Asian markets are factors that collectively are leading to strategic alliances. Some of these new working relationships take the form of ownership stakes, but others take the form of contractual relationships for specific services. Together, these changes help to make the banking industry a dynamic, changing field with the growing opportunities across industry lines and national boundaries.

Within the United States

With permission by federal regulators to offer securities services, U.S. commercial banks have formed alliances with securities firms and increased the general level of activity in securities trading. This trend is evident in regional banking circles as well as in the money center institutions.

Mutual Funds

A joint venture between a bank and a securities firm helps move the bank in the direction of a full-service provider of financial products. The greatest asset a commercial bank possesses is its relationship with customers, a characteristic that enables it to cross-sell products. As a group, however, commercial banks were precluded from engaging in securities transactions for many years and, thus, many have not developed the full set of skills appropriate in the securities industry.

In forming such an alliance, a bank must carefully guard its reputation for being a safe haven for investing. In this connection, guidelines were developed in 1993 to protect the bank customer. After federal regulators issued advisory guidelines in July, six banking associations formulated similar guidelines in September.[34] It is suggested that banks locate the areas designated for mutual fund sales away from teller windows so that customers do not confuse FDIC-insured products with mutual funds which do not protect investors from loss of principal. Also, customers should be informed clearly that mutual funds are not traditional deposit instruments and should be asked to sign a statement to acknowledge their awareness of this difference. Such guidelines are particularly important in view of the popularity of mutual funds, with sales through banks amounting to over $40 billion in 1992 (or 14 percent of the total sales of $300 billion).

Clearly, if a joint venture between a bank and a securities firm goes well, the bank has gained a potentially lucrative fee-income generating operation. If it is does not go well, for instance, if the mutual fund partner becomes invasive and uses client lists in ways that create internal friction, the benefits may not justify the costs. If the partnership falls apart, then the bank has wasted valuable time and resources in an arena with little future prospects and has also damaged its image in the financial community. Thus, selecting the right partner is critical.

IDS and First Bank System (FBS) formed a joint venture to provide financial planning and products through two First Bank offices in Albert Lea and Owatonna, Minnesota. IDS is owned by American Express Company and concentrates primarily on financial planning, with more than 7300 financial planners in 50 states. The arrangement is to provide IDS with an attractive sales channel. FBS hopes that the arrangement will help it develop a sharper sales focus and lead to greater revenues. In the Albert Lea office, an IDS licensed representative will offer IDS products while, in the Owatonna office, a sales representative from FBS will offer the same set of products. The results of the pilot program will help determine the direction of future efforts.

---

[34] The six banking associations that drafted the guidelines are Consumer Bankers Association, Independent Bankers Association of America, American Bankers Association, Association of Reserve City Bankers, National Bankers Association, and Savings and Community Bankers of America.

Chemical Investment Services is a joint venture between Chemical Banking Corporation and Liberty Financial Services, a subsidiary of Liberty Mutual Insurance. Products offered to customers are The Hanover Funds (a family of nine funds managed by Chemical affiliates), five Liberty Financial funds, third-party mutual funds, annuities, stocks, and bonds. Liberty Financial Bank Group acts as broker-dealer with Chemical focusing on customer delivery. Over time, Chemical Investment Services is expected to grow from its current sales force level of 60 seasoned securities representatives to more than 300, with 190 in Chemical branches in the New York area.

Bank of America (formerly NationsBank) teamed up with Dean Witter in what may be one of the most ambitious combinations to-date. There are hundreds of "investment officers" in specific Bank of America offices, with half from each organization. The bank concentrates on Dean Witter's mutual funds but also sells other funds, depending on customer demand. The characteristics that attracted the bank to the brokerage firm are Dean Witter's operational systems, software support, and sales experience. Bank of America has even discussed syndicating the arrangement with other banks.

Securities Trading and BankAmerica

BankAmericahas been no less aggressive in its approach to securities trading. With the goal of expanding this activity, BankAmerica owns Chicago Research and Trading (CRT). The $225 million acquisition brings to BankAmerica a primary government securities dealer and an experienced trader in options and futures contracts.

BankAmerica can offer its clients a wider array of products through which financial risk can be managed. CRT is one of Chicago's biggest and most respected futures and options traders and is also experienced in currency swaps, forward-rate agreements, and interest-rate options--derivative products that many bank clients find particularly useful.

BankAmerica also uses CRT's expertise to manage the risk within its own $618-billion balance sheet. Its securities investment portfolio is in excess of $70 billion, composed largely of government bonds and mortgage-backed securities.

CRT employs approximately 800 people and has 150 memberships in 19 exchanges worldwide. It trades roughly 150,000 contracts daily with an average aggregate face value of $10 billion. Its overall strategy is to lock in small, but low-risk profits by capturing arbitrage profits in different markets. It trading expertise should add to NationsBank bottom line in the trading division.

Regional Expansion

BankAmerica

The alliances of BankAmerica have not been limited to improved product offerings but have also revealed the objective of wide regional expansion, with a ranking of second largest U.S. commercial bank. BankAmerica has the largest branch network in the country and dominates the Southeast and the West.

Before BankAmerica and NationsBank merged, the predecessor institutions included NCNB (North Carolina National Bank), Sovran Bank of Virginia, and Citizens & Southern of Georgia. Before NationsBank was formed, NCNB had been the largest bank in North Carolina since 1979. In 1982, NCNB became the first non-Florida bank to expand its retail banking into Florida when it purchased First National Bank of Lake City. During the next two years, it bought banks in Boca Raton, Tampa, Miami, and Bradenton. The acquisition of Pan American Bank in Miami in 1985 added another 51 offices. By 1988, NCNB was the 4th largest bank in Florida.

The bank's interstate presence was expanded by purchases of Southern National Bankshares, Inc. (Atlanta), Bankers Trust of South Carolina (122 branches statewide), and Prince William Bank of Dumfries (Virginia). By 1986, it was the first bank to operate in 5 southern states. The following year, it bought CentraBank (Baltimore) to bring the number of southern states to 6.

The asset base of NCNB doubled in 1988 when FDIC selected the bank to manage the banks that had been part of failed First RepublicBank Corporation, formerly the largest commercial bank in Texas. NCNB had been permitted to buy 20 percent of the institutions in 1987; by 1989 the remaining share belonged to NCNB. National Bancshares of San Antonio became part of the organization in 1990.

Also in 1990, Citizens and Southern (Georgia) and Sovran (Virginia) merged into C&S/Sovran. The following year, NCNB took over C&S/Sovran to become NationsBank. With a presence in North Carolina, South Carolina, Georgia, Florida, Texas, Maryland, and Virginia and $7 billion in Tier I capital, the selection of the name NationsBank is certainly appropriate.

With the merger of NationsBank and BankAmerica, BankAmerica positined itself for the relaxation of federal branching restrictions. At the same time, the bank has expanded into those activities that will help it remain competitive in both corporate finance and retail banking.

Banc One

With its $262 billion in assets and $20 billion in Tier I capital, there are few U.S. banking institutions that have a higher ranking (in terms of capital) than Banc One Corporation—Citigroup, BankAmerica Corporation, and Chase Manhattan Corporation.

In 1929, the two Columbus banks Commercial National and City National Bank of Commerce, merged to form City National Bank and Trust. John H. McCoy was the bank's first president. His son John G. McCoy took over in 1958 and shortly thereafter started to break with tradition. In 1966, the bank introduced the first Visa credit card outside of California (then BankAmericard). McCoy formed First Banc Group in 1967, a holding company of which City National was a subsidiary. Then in 1968, the company bought Farmers Savings and Trust of Mansfield, Ohio. By 1985, the holding company owned a total of 44 Ohio banks.

In a 1977 alliance, First Bank Group was designated as the bank to manage the Cash Management Account (CMA) for Merrill Lynch. This innovation brought together a retail brokerage account, a checking account, and a debit card, representing an aggressive post-Glass-Steagall combination of services.

In 1979, First Banc Group changed its name to Banc One and all bank subsidiaries included Bank One in their names.[35] When the third generation McCoy, John B., took over the reins in 1984, the emergence of multistate regional agreements with respect to bank acquisitions had begun. Banc One expanded into Indiana, Kentucky, Michigan, and Wisconsin. With FDIC guarantees against loss, Banc One purchased the loans of 20 of the branches of MCorp (Texas), paying $34 million for $11 billion in assets

---

[35] The holding company assumed the name Banc One, with a "c" because Ohio law restricts the use of the word bank.

($2.5 billion of which were troubled). In 1991, Illinois was added to the list of states in which Banc One operates.

Early on, Banc One grew by acquiring smaller banks, consolidating back-office operations, and mixing local control with regional marketing power. The company continues to stress retail banking, quickly taking advantage of technological advances such as ATMs and home banking systems. With its technology, Banc One maintains a master file that records which products each customer is likely to buy. Its corporate clientele is the middle market. The bank's overall strategy involves conservative lending, innovative technology, dedicated customer service, and mergers with other banks.

In identifying potential candidates for merger, Banc One follows certain guidelines:

- Never merge with a peer.
- Do not buy a bank more than one-third the size of the existing Banc One organization.
- Leave the existing management in place.
- Allow each bank to make its own decisions in a decentralized fashion.

These decentralized operations are coordinated through a system of common products, technology, and monthly reporting requirements.

As the result of these strategic alliances, Banc One's 1999 asset base of $262 billion is more than eight times its 1990 level. With locations in Ohio, Kentucky, Indiana, Illinois, Michigan, Wisconsin, and Texas, the Banc One presence now reaches from the Great Lakes to the Gulf of Mexico.

PNC Financial Corporation

PNC has the twelfth largest bank capital base in the United States, totaling $5.5 billion. Its asset base is $77 billion. The First National Bank of Pittsburgh was one of the first banks chartered in 1863 under the National Bank Act passed in the same year. The bank merged with Second National Bank of Pittsburgh in 1913. By 1921, the institution had also merged with Peoples National Bank (Pittsburgh).

In the 1940s, the bank made strategic acquisitions to establish a strong trust business, acquiring Pittsburgh Trust, Sewickley Valley Trust, and Monongahela Trust. The name of the bank was then changed to Pittsburgh National. In 1965 the bank entered the credit card business and joined the Bankamericard program in 1969. The holding company Pittsburgh National Corporation was formed in 1968 and a series of holding company acquisitions followed: Pittsburgh National Discount (commercial paper), PINACO (insurance on commercial loans), Pittsburgh National Leasing (lease financing), and Pittsburgh National Life (credit life, health, and accident reinsurance). These acquisitions enabled the bank to enter nonbank financial activities that were permitted within the scope of bank holding companies.

In 1983 another strategic merger strengthened the institution's position in money management and trust operations. Pittsburgh National combined with Provident National of Philadelphia to become PNC Corporation. Acquisitions followed in other parts of Pennsylvania, Kentucky, Ohio, New Jersey, and Delaware. PNC appears to have found its niche, a strong and diverse regional banking presence with a diversified scope of services.

European Alliances and Investment Banking

Banks have retrenched from their overseas activities because of international and domestic loan losses and because of more stringent capital requirements, there remain a number of opportunities that have not been completely exploited. In order to realize some of these opportunities, it is necessary to form alliances--not necessarily mergers, but instead other working relationships that capitalize on the competitive advantages of each of the partners.

There are certain elements that will be critical in terms of the ability of a financial institution to adequately serve institutional clients, which are an increasingly important segment of investors. Because of the extent of new issues on a global basis, one of these elements is an *investment banking* capacity.

Bilateral lending, that is, a borrower receiving funding through one institution only and eliminating the need for a syndicate, can be risky business. Attempting to compete in bilateral lending, a bank usually must go head-to-head with a borrower's relationship bank. Such attempts generally will be successful only if the bank offers some form of concession--either on price or on the covenant contained in the loan agreement. Those banks that make such concessions are actually placing lower credit into their investment portfolios which can affect the market as a whole. From the borrower's perspective, these concessions may be misleading and the borrower may be disappointed in subsequent financings. In later attempts to access mainstream funding, the borrower may discover that the terms it has come to anticipate (because of bilateral concessions) are unrealistic.

Furthermore, market analysts believe that the demand for syndicated loans is likely to increase as corporate and sovereign borrowers come forward. The top loan arrangers in the Euro syndicated loan market include five U.S. institutions: J.P. Morgan, Citicorp, Bankers Trust, Chase Manhattan, and BankAmerica. Sovereign borrowers are major bond issuers and have great demand for financing. Here, the combination of relationship banking and strong research is critical. Specific steps can be taken to improve an institution's likelihood of being given a mandate, that is, being selected as lead manager of a sovereign bond issue:

- *Understand the borrower's program.* This requires that a bank understand the sovereign's financing goals and legal constraints. There is a general trend for sovereign issuers to provide more information so that institutions can submit more informed bids.
- *Determine whether the sovereign is attempting to actively manage its liabilities.* Some issuers have become sensitive to the currency mix and timing of their liabilities. The successful bids will require an understanding of such strategic decisions as well as the more customary funding-level requirements.
- *Be prepared to offer liability management advice.* Not all sovereigns rely on their underwriters for liability management advice, but most will take note of the availability of this service.
- *Be prepared to assist with any credit-rating difficulties.* When borrowers have less than a AAA credit rating, the presentation of the deal to rating agencies can be a critical phase of the offering. The time and energy spent in research and documentation can be instrumental in obtaining the highest possible credit rating for the sovereign issuer.
- *Be attentive to the aftermarket.* When bonds are issued, the performance of the bonds in the secondary market will affect later issuances by the borrower. In addition, a sovereign may expect the firm to which it awards the mandate to make a market in the bonds.
- *Remember that relationships count.* Unless a firm has established some sort of relationship with a sovereign, it will be difficult to obtain the mandate, or, in some cases, to even be invited to bid.

- *Don't neglect the competitive issues.* While relationships are important for initial consideration, ultimately the bid with the most attractive terms and services will be most competitive.
- *Have the ability to offer a truly global issue.* The bonds that can be promoted in several markets will be the most successful. This means that the underwriting firm must have established alliances (through its own offices or syndication relationships) to offer an international presence.

If these steps are taken, a financial institution can significantly increase its chances of being selected to lead a sovereign bond flotation.

There is also a growing trend toward direct equity investments, including depository receipt transactions--ADRs, IDRs, or GDRs. *American depository receipts (ADRs)* are negotiable certificates issued by a U.S. bank for shares of stock issued by a foreign corporation. The securities are held in a custodial account, either at the issuing bank or an agent. ADRs are registered with the Securities and Exchange Commission, give the holder the same rights as shareholders, are priced in dollars, and trade in either over-the-counter or organized exchanges. Among the 10 most actively traded ADRs are eight from European countries:

Company	Country	Exchange
Glaxo Holdings	U.K.	NYSE
Hanson	U.K.	NYSE
British Petroleum	U.K.	NYSE
Saatchi & Saatchi	U.K.	NYSE
Telefonica Nacional de España	Spain	NYSE
Wellcome	U.K.	NYSE
Memorex	Netherlands	NASDAQ
SmithKline Beecham	U.K.	NYSE

The remaining two are issues of Telefonos de Mexico (Telmex), one traded on the NYSE (New York Stock Exchange) and the other on NASDAQ (National Association of Securities Dealers Automated Quotations).

An *International Depository Receipt (IDR)* is the non-U.S.-dollar equivalent of an ADR that is sold in Europe. *Global Depository Receipts*

(GDRs) are sold in both the United States and Europe. In the case of a GDR, the shares are easily exchanged between different markets.

Greater China and Alliances with Western Banks

Greater China is Southern China, Hong Kong, and Taiwan. Many Chinese banks have overextended themselves to meet the demands of capital formation and, in some cases, property speculation. There has been a major construction boom in the country's coastal regions and this construction has been financed largely by the banks.

Zhu Rongji, premier of the People's Republic of China and the former governor of the People's Bank of China (the central bank), was charged with containing inflation and with reforming the financial system. The People's Bank of China has enjoyed its current status as a western-style central bank only since 1984. Because of lax controls prior to Zhu's assumption of the governor's position, it was estimated that actual nonperforming loans of specific banks ranged anywhere from 3 to 45 percent of total loan portfolios. Furthermore, many banks operated nonbanking financial institutions, such as leasing and consumer credit companies, to escape the scrutiny of the People's Bank of China altogether.

In order to reform the system, Zhu directed the People's Bank of China to act merely as a supervisory and regulatory agency rather than, as was previously the case, a hybrid between a commercial and a central bank. Then the specialized banks were freed from politically motivated, but unprofitable, loans. This encourages more fundamentally sound investments by these institutions.

In the meantime, Zhu set down rules to reign in the excesses of the system, incluidng the following measures:

- No new loans to nonbanking financial institutions.
- Recall of Rmb100 billion in such loans.[36]
- Increased savings deposits by all banks.
- Visits and inspections of regional banking offices by enforcement teams of the People's Bank of China.

Zhu set the tone for the reformed banking system of China.

---

36. Renminbi (Rmb) is Chinese currency.

The attraction for commercial banks is considerable. The recent investment wave has been spurred by the synergies created in this region. China contributes a low-cost labor pool and abundant land resources. Hong Kong is a source of marketing and financial skills. Taiwan is a base for technology transfer.

The intent of the Chinese government is clearly to encourage development of this economic arrangement. For example, in 1993, the Beijing government remained silent when Japanese banks took significant steps to increase their presence in Taiwan. Previously, Beijing had attempted to block the expansion of Japanese banks in Taiwan because the People's Republic claims sovereignty over the country. Only Dai-Ichi Kangyo Bank had maintained a Taiwanese branch. Recently, the Tokai Bank requested a license for a representative office and Bank of Tokyo requested that its representative office license be upgraded to a full service branch. Beijing's muted reaction to these applications signalled other banks from Japan and elsewhere that such alliances would not jeopardize their existing relationships with the People's Republic of China.

In 1992, China liberalized the permissible locations for foreign bank branches. In addition to the five Special Zones of Shenzhen, Zhuhai, Hainan, Xiamen, and Shantou, another eight cities may now be the home of foreign banks:

- Shanghai
- Dalian
- Tianjin
- Qingdao
- Nanjing
- Ningbo
- Fuzhou
- Guangzhou

At the end of 1995, 102 representative offices of foreign institutions operated in China. In addition, a number of foreign bank branches have been opened. Shanghai alone had 42 foreign bank branches in mid-1996.

Foreign banks are having a significant impact on the Chinese market. The introduction of bank cards will likely lead to an international-style network for the acceptance of bank cards in China. Currently, stores and restaurants accept only those cards issued by the banks with which they do business. Government authorities have issued directives to build interbank networks in 12 cities that will authorize and settle card transactions. Both Visa and MasterCard of the United States are vying to help develop this initiative. Involvement by foreign banks will be in the best interest of the Chinese financial system as China is plagued by chronic shortages of currency and a mounting problem with counterfeiting.

Chinese authorities also hope that foreign institutions will help develop Shanghai into the financial center of Asia. Specifically, the PBOC has permitted nine foreign banks to conduct business in renminbi on a limited basis beginning in late 1996. Permitted renminbi business includes deposits, loans, payment settlements, security for loans (loan guarantees), bonds issued by the government, and other business individually authorized by the PBOC. The condition for doing so is opening sub-branches in the Pudong development district of Shanghai or in the cities of Tianjin, Dalian, and Guangzhou. Pudong is slated to be the new financial district of Shanghai. As of mid-1997, the nine banks with permission to conduct renminbi business were Citibank, Hong Kong and Shanghai Banking Corporation, Bank of Tokyo-Mitsubishi, the Industrial Bank of Japan, Sanwa Bank, Dai-Ichi Kangyo, International Bank of Paris, Standard Chartered Bank, and Banque Indosuez.

By overcoming many of the previous political barriers to trade and finance, Beijing is clearing the way to sustained growth in Greater China. Such economic vitality and pragmatic approaches to business are attracting the attention of international banks which hope to capitalize on the need for a more modern Chinese banking system.

The most promising strategic alliances in the People's Republic of China that can be established at this time are in the areas of the payments system, cash management, syndicated loans, and securities underwriting. As the banking and securities markets are further strengthened and liberalized, these opportunities will continue to grow, as well as access to the 1.2 billion potential customers in the Chinese retail market.

Conclusion

International skills will be increasingly important as cross-border alliances form in Europe and Asia. Many of the definitions of commercial banking are, indeed, changing. Nevertheless, commercial banks have both the skills and the ingenuity to successfully compete in the evolving markets of global finance.

Selected References

The Banker 1000, special edition of *The Banker*, July 1999.

Barnathan, Joyce and Matt Forney. "Between Reform and a Hard Line: China's Economic Czar is Battling the Old Guard and Local Capitalists," *Business Week*, September 6, 1993.

Bennett, Robert. "Forging a New Bank at PNC," *United States Banker*, July 1993, pp. 22-28.

Bennett, Rosemary. "Universal Banks Play the Investor Card," *Euromoney*, May 1993 supplement, pp. 71-80.

Chai, Alan, Alta Campbell, and Patrick J. Spain, Editors. *Hoover's Handbook of World Business 1993*, The Reference Press, Austin, Texas, 1993.

"Crédit Lyonnais--Europe's Most Expansionist Bank," *Financial Revolution in Europe II*, Lafferty Publications, Dublin, 1992, pp. 258-263.

Dyer, Geoff. "The Going Gets Easier as Spreads Narrow," *Euromoney*, March 1993 supplement, pp. 2-28.

Fitch, Thomas P. *Dictionary of Banking Terms*, Barron's, Hauppauge, New York, 1990.

"French Top Acquisitions League in EC," *European Banker*, August 23, 1993, p. 5.

"The Great Divide in European Research," *Euromoney*, September 1993, pp. 372-390.

Hagger, Euan. "Why the Market's Dinosaurs are Back in Fashion," *Euromoney*, August 1993, pp. 65-70.

"Here Comes Hugh (Again)," *United States Banker*, July 1993, p. 6.

"How to Sell to Sovereigns," *Euromoney*, September 1993, pp. 46-58.

Jackson, Ted. "NationsBank Buys Big-League Status," *Euromoney*, April 1993, pp.71-72.

Leung, Julia. "Beijing Remains Silent as Japanese Banks Move Into Taiwan," *Asian Wall Street Journal*, February 15, 1993.

Loong, Pauline. "Can the Economy Achieve a Soft Landing?" *Euromoney*, August 1993, pp. 41-42.

Marray, Michael. "Public Issuance Overtakes Private Placements," *Euromoney*, April 1993, pp. 117-119.

Marshall, Jeffrey. "Banks and Brokers Take a Leap," *United States Banker*, August 1993, pp. 13-14,63.

McGill, Peter. "Shanghai Bids to Become a Top Financial Centre," *Euromoney*, April 1993, pp.57-62.

Miller, Richard B. *Citicorp: The Story of a Bank in Crisis*, McGraw-Hill, Inc, New York, 1993.

"Retail Market Beckons (Country Survey: Germany)," *European Banker*, August 10, 1993, p. 10.

Robinson, David. "Putting the Shareholder First," *European Banker*, May 21, 1993, pp. 9-10.

Robinson, David. "To Stay or Go (UK Banks in Europe)," *European Banker*, August 23, 1993, pp. 8-10.

Schmerken, Ivy. "Germany's Equity Markets Recharge Their Batteries," *Wall Street and Technology*, vol. 11, no. 2 (1993), pp. 32-35.

Shale, Tony. "Foreign Banks Scramble to Win Chinese Business," *Euromoney*, August 1993, pp. 38-40.

Shale, Tony. "Scramble Starts to Win Share of State Sell-offs," *Euromoney*, February 1993, pp. 80-81.

Shale, Tony. "Zhu Rongji's Big Gamble," *Euromoney*, August 1993, pp. 32-36.

Shepperd, Rosie. "The Investor Side of New Issues," *Euromoney*, July 1993, pp. 75-77.

Shirreff, David. "Assault on Frankfurt--Part Two," *Euromoney*, August 1993, pp. 54-60.

"Who's Selling What: The Global Picture," *Euromoney*, July 1993, pp. 114-125.